"*Through a blending of science and my........ Hardwired to Heaven by Joan Cerio takes us on a journey to new understandings of yourself, your connection to the divine, and ultimately to living as a co-creator. Joan helps us to see the interrelationship between our physical heart, its center point, and that of the unified field of the Universe. In this work she teaches us to light the spark of coherence with that of creation. I recommend this to anyone who wants to further their studies into science and mysticism.*"

— **DAVID BENNETT**, Co-author of *Voyage of Purpose: Spiritual Wisdom from Near Death back to Life*, **www.DharmaTalks.com**

"*Complex insights from the minds of our greatest modern thinkers, on the nature of the great and mysterious elephant in our darkened room, are made simple and understandable by Joan Cerio in* **Hardwired to Heaven**. *Revealing an emerging world view from molecule to galaxy and back to the core of the soul, this book clearly models a vision of our personal relationship with the Great Mystery illuminating all our hearts.*"

— **PETER CHAMPOUX**, author of *Gaia Matrix*

green press
INITIATIVE

Findhorn Press is committed to preserving ancient forests and natural resources. We elected to print this title on 30% post consumer recycled paper, processed chlorine free. As a result, for this printing, we have saved:

4 Trees (40' tall and 6-8" diameter)
2 Million BTUs of Total Energy
302 Pounds of Greenhouse Gases
1,639 Gallons of Wastewater
110 Pounds of Solid Waste

Findhorn Press made this paper choice because our printer, Thomson-Shore, Inc., is a member of Green Press Initiative, a nonprofit program dedicated to supporting authors, publishers, and suppliers in their efforts to reduce their use of fiber obtained from endangered forests.

For more information, visit www.greenpressinitiative.org

Environmental impact estimates were made using the Environmental Defense Paper Calculator. For more information visit: www.papercalculator.org.

MIX

Paper from responsible sources

FSC® C013483

HARDWIRED
TO
HEAVEN

Download Your Divinity
Through Your Heart
and Create
Your Deepest Desires

JOAN CERIO

 FINDHORN PRESS

ISBN 978-1-84409-463-9

Edited by Michael Hawkins
Cover design by Richard Crookes
Interior design by Damian Keenan
Illustrations by Damian Keenan
(except for Figures 1, 15, 28, 29, 30, 31)

Printed and bound in the USA

Published by
Findhorn Press
117-121 High Street,
Forres IV36 1AB,
Scotland, UK

t +44 (0)1309 690582
f +44 (0)131 777 2711
e info@findhornpress.com
www.findhornpress.com

Dedication

*I dedicate this book to the tenacity of the human spirit
to know itself and to those who have mastered it.*

Acknowledgements

Researching, writing, and living this book has been a labor of love for nine years. Throughout those years, many people have come into my life and gifted me with insights, inspiration, and information for this book.

In particular, I would like to thank Mark David Gerson, writing coach, screenwriter, and author. He was instrumental in starting me on my writing journey, coaching me along the way, offering words of encouragement, editing the book, being one of my dearest friends, and showing me what the love of writing and tenacity can do. He continues to be an inspiration for me, and many others.

For all of the phone conversations, emails, research, strokes of insight, love, and laughter, I am grateful to my twin flame, Steven Pawlak. I am so grateful we found each other again in this life to co-create even more wondrous things.

For all of her support, whether it is an intuitive insight about a basilica or introducing me to her friends who provided more insight for my book, for sharing a good laugh, and for all of her encouragement, I am so grateful to Sue Hirschberger. Thank you, Sue, for finding me again in this lifetime. I cherish our friendship.

For all of her research, wisdom, words of support, and friendship, I send my gratitude and love to my soul sister, Karen Weaver.

To Sedona, Arizona and the many friends I made there, whose energy and wisdom had prepared me for writing and living this book, enormous gratitude and love.

To Sandie Hensley, my Sedona surrogate mother, what would I have done without you?! Thank you for always opening your home to me whenever I returned to Sedona.

To Gold Beach, Oregon, and my friends that made my stay there possible… many thanks. It was amidst the energy of the Rogue River flowing into the vast Pacific Ocean that I was inspired to write the chapter on blood and water and the information about gold. Your beauty and the friends I made there will always remain in my heart.

To all of my family and friends who have supported me on this journey, even when the journey took me thousands of miles away, I am forever grateful. I am especially grateful to my sisters Janet Lottermoser and Jean Halpern, who have provided the place, time, and sustenance to complete this book. You are my angels and I love you.

Most of all, I am grateful to the god that I AM for following my heart and creating this book. May it inspire others to live as the god that they are.

Joan Cerio

Contents

Contents

List of Illustrations

Preface

I am in love with life. From that day in high school biology class when, after learning that we form from a single cell, I looked down at myself and literally jumped in my seat, I began my quest to understand life. More importantly, I longed to know about the creator of life. What was God like? How does God think? Most of all, who am I in relation to God?

In my search for answers, I fell in love with the spiritual. I would often visit my church and sit in the front pew and pray, or rather, talk to the statues of Jesus, Mary, and Joseph. Somewhere deep in my soul, I knew they were my equals. Somehow, I recognized that the wisdom of Jesus lay in *my* heart. Didn't his statue-self point to his heart as if to tell me that the key to all of my longing resided there?

After my parents persuaded me not to become a nun, I returned to my first love and studied biology. During my early adult years, I either taught science or worked in health and healing professions. My soul longed for more. So much so, that I ultimately left everything behind – my job, my family, and my home, to devote my life to studying the metaphysical.

Those of you who know Sedona also know how its energy can first entice you to stay and then, just as suddenly, expel you as though you have overstayed your welcome, only to draw you back again. For five years, Sedona and I had that kind of on and off relationship, with a year being our longest continuous time together. I learned much from its land, people, and energy. Even more importantly, I learned about myself. Through my many experiences there and since, I am now able to answer the question, "Who am I?" and I now understand at deeper levels much of the magic of life.

My most recent stay in Sedona, in 2009, was, by far, the most magical. While there, I asked to be shown who I really am, my essential self. After a series of unambiguous happenings, I was shown just that through a unique and unusual download – an alchemical recipe of remembering – that went something like this:

1) Take one krybryone tektite stone activation, mix in one group sweat-lodge meditation, and stir.
2) Meet your twin flame.
3) Add a trip to Chaco Canyon, and shake.
4) Read *Unveiled Mysteries (Original)* by Godfrey Ray King and pay particular attention to the last page.
5) Meditate with gem stones specially chosen by your twin flame. Stir well. Stir again.
6) Research, letting your intuition guide the process.
7) Pay close attention to the results of the research, and heed all resulting messages.
8) Allow yourself to be swept up in all the energy of the experiences.
9) Listen carefully to what others say to you.
10) Allow all ingredients to marinate… and integrate!

Voilá! One divine download!

So who am I after all this, you ask? Read on, and you will more than likely find out. Perhaps the more important question, though, is "Who are *you*?" You will find answers to that question, too, as you move through this book and log into your connection to your divine nature.

Here is a hint: The purpose of God or of any god/goddess is to create. Through these pages, you will discover how you as a human are becoming a god – an enlightened being with the power to create. With an open heart and mind, and a commitment to download your divinity, you can log into your heart's connection to creation and live as the god that you are.

It's time to begin the journey. Turn the page and read on!

Introduction

*H*ardwired to Heaven: Download Your Divinity Through Your Heart *and Create Your Deepest Desires* is not just another book on manifesting – it is a prerequisite for the School of Creation. There are many books that claim to reveal the secret formula for manifesting. While they all contain valuable information, they omit this essential fact: Creating is the natural result of *downloading*, and *living*, as the god that you are. Only after you vibrate at the frequency of your god self and entrain to the energy of creation, can you command the particles of creation.

You are about to embark not only on a journey to the heart of creation, but also to the heart of who you are. You will learn about the heart's sacred connection to the divine and how to login to access the valuable information inside. Everything you create in your life comes through this divine connection. It is only after we transcend the depths of our heart that we can download and live our divinity.

Hardwired to Heaven is a blending of my two true loves: science and mysticism. Although it is written for the novice scientist, it is not for the faint-of-heart mystic. Science without spirituality is hollow; spirituality without science is incomplete.

Reading *Hardwired to Heaven* is like climbing a mountain: As you ascend each plateau (chapter), you will gain the understanding necessary to reach the summit, where a pot of creative gold is waiting for you. Before you reach the metaphysical, you must first traverse the scientific information that is its foundation. On that part of the journey, you will learn the science behind using your heart's electromagnetic field to create. As on any journey, it is important that you allow time for each portion (chapter) to seep in and integrate. At the summit – the end of the book – you will discover the practical tools that will enhance your ability to manifest, as well as step-by-step instructions on how to create using your heart's electromagnetic field. Because the effectiveness of these techniques increases with some understanding of the underlying science, I encourage you to resist any temptation to skip ahead.

The other reason why I include quite a bit of science here is because I want you to catch a glimpse of how miraculous your body and heart are, how precious and important water is, and how connected you are to all of creation. My hope is that after finishing this book, you will fall in love with your heart, and with water, as I have.

Sprinkled throughout the science are my own theories. Some of these theories, along with other insights, came to me through meditations, automatic writings, and dreams.

In my first book, *In the Key of Life: An Activational Journey to the Soul*, my goal was to help your *mind* integrate the truth of who you are. With *Hardwired to Heaven*, my objective is to guide you to the next step — *living* as the co-creator that you are — by providing you with the knowledge, wisdom, and tools to create your gifts for humanity through your *heart,* your connection to the divine. While the foundational information will remain useful, the steps to creating will only be needed until your level of mastery and vibration increases to the point that you are able to manifest instantaneously by thinking *and* desiring from your heart. Now that should be motivation enough to keep reading!

One final note: I make numerous references throughout the book to Jesus and the Bible as religious examples because I was raised Catholic and I am more familiar with this religion than any other. I do not espouse any particular religion nor do I practice any religion. All religions have truths and all lead us back home when we practice their masters' intended interpretations of their teachings.

It is unfortunate that a small group of men who knew the power of the truth decided to twist it and keep it from the masses (pun intended!).

CHAPTER ONE

Timing Is Everything

I wonder if I've been changed in the night? Let me think.
Was I the same when I got up this morning?
I almost think I can remember feeling a little different.
But if I'm not the same, the next question is,
'Who in the world am I?' Ah, that's the great puzzle!

— *LEWIS CARROLL*
ALICE'S ADVENTURES IN WONDERLAND, 1865

Fast-forward about 150 years from Alice's time and we all find ourselves down a version of her rabbit hole. The Maya call this the lifetime of change. I like to refer to it as the lifetime full of lifetimes of change. How many "lifetimes" have you lived within this lifetime? Think back to who you were just a year ago and I think you will get my point. The collective alarm clock is still going off even though infamous 2012 has come and gone. The new age has become the now age.

Many indigenous peoples predicted this Shift. The Hopi, a Native American tribe located in northern Arizona, has predicted that when our minds and our hearts become separated and are no longer one, Mother Earth will heal herself through catastrophic change. After this, we will enter the peaceful fifth world of consciousness. In this next world, the Hopi say, it will be important to maintain balance between our mind, our heart, and the earth because our thoughts, desires, and actions will all happen simultaneously. What we feel in our heart will be made immediately manifest in the physical world.

The Hopi's prediction that manifesting our hearts' desires will manifest at the speed of thought is intimately connected to the magnetic field of the earth. The strength of the earth's magnetic field has been steadily decreasing since the first measurements were recorded in 1829. The earth's magnetic field is a depository of human memory, similar to how the magnetic stripe on the back of a credit card holds information. As the intensity decreases – some say it will ultimately zero out – the field's ability to maintain the integrity of this information also decreases.

This zeroing-out of Earth's magnetic field is like hitting the master reset button for humanity, providing a supportive environment in which to release old belief systems, past patterns, and karmic connections that no longer resonate with the earth's and our higher vibratory rate. At the same time, as the magnetic field decreases both our ability to manifest and the rate of manifestation increases.

Lastly, as the intensity of the magnetic field of the earth decreases, the rate at which the earth vibrates increases from 7.8 to 13 Hz. Since our hearts' electromagnetic field is connected with that of the earth's, our vibratory rate increases as well.

As the earth's electromagnetic field approaches extremely low levels, it may also create the perfect environment for cell regeneration. Dr. Carlo Ventura, an epigenetic researcher, recently discovered that exposure to extremely low frequency magnetic fields can induce adult human cells to become pluripotent, meaning that they become stem cells that can differentiate into cardiac, neural, or skeletal muscle cells. In other words, exposure to extremely low frequency electromagnetic fields can regenerate heart, brain, and muscle cells (Ventura and McCraty 2013).

The Ancients knew of the interconnectedness of everything, including our connection with Mother Earth. Every aspect of our being changes as our vibration increases: physically, emotionally, mentally, and spiritually. Codes within our DNA that have been dormant are now activating. Thought processes and habits are changing. Lower frequency emotions, such as anger and fear, are coming up to be cleared. Our chakra system, and aura, become harmonic with this higher vibration.

Another change related to the earth's magnetic field is at our doorstep. This change involves the coinciding of the earth's weakening magnetic field and the strengthening of solar cycle 24, which may have peaked in 2013. But not all solar physicists are convinced that the worst is over. In a March 1, 2013 Science@NASA Newsletter, Dr. Tony Phillips wrote that solar physicists speculate that this solar cycle may have two peaks and the second peak may occur in 2015 (NASA 2013).

Solar activity, which increased dramatically in 2012, may have precipitated super storm Sandy that battered the east coast of the United States. The last time the earth experienced similar solar wind intensity was in 1859. Then, telegraph poles were rendered inoperative. We were much less reliant on technology in 1859, so the effects of that solar wind event were not as dramatic as what may occur in 2015. Some say that all satellites, power grids, electrical and electromagnetic equipment, and various forms of communication will be virtually destroyed unless we prepare now. What makes this solar cycle so intense is that the sun's poles flipped, causing the sun to send out a burst of energy toward the earth at a time when her magnetic field defenses are low.

The sun may not be the only celestial body to experience a pole reversal. Data shows that the magnetic field of the earth decreases prior to a pole reversal. The earth has experienced numerous pole reversals, about one every half a million years. The last polar shift happened about 780,000 years ago, making the earth ripe for another reversal. Scientists agree that magnetic north is migrating at a faster speed than it did in the 1800s. According to a September 2010 article on Phys.org, geophysicists Bogue and Glen published an article refuting the prior evidence that the process of shifting the poles happens over thousands of years. Scientists now have data to support that a pole reversal happens over a much shorter period of time and that we can expect another reversal in the near future (Phys.org 2010).

Large-magnitude earthquakes, such as in New Zealand and Japan, have already shifted the earth's axis and magnetic north. When the poles actually trade places, there is a short period of time where the geomagnetic field resets itself and is nonexistent. Perhaps this explains the three days of darkness that various traditions have predicted. This solar cycle and decreasing geomagnetic field may precipitate such an event.

The Maya are most noted for their calendar and predictions for this time, which were based in part on the sun. Excellent astronomers, the Maya knew about the movement of the planets, the sun, and the galactic center. They were able to predict the current galactic alignment zone that modern astronomers have calculated to occur from 1980 through 2016. Galactic alignment occurs as a result of the precession of equinoxes. This precession is caused by the wobble of the earth on its axis. This celestially slight movement alters the position of the equinoxes and solstices by one degree every

71.5 years. From our perspective on Earth the sun is one half degree wide. Doing the math, it will take the December solstice sun about 36 years to move across the galactic equator. This alignment happens once approximately every 26,000 years and may have been what the Maya were pointing to with the December 21, 2012 end date of their long count calendar.

The Mayan Calendars are more than just a measure of time; they are a measure of human consciousness. The much-publicized Mayan Calendar ended in December 2012 and we have just begun a new one. According to Ian Lungold, a student of the Mayan Calendar, and Carl Calleman, an expert in the previous Mayan Calendar, the calendar consisted of nine waves or cycles. Each cycle built upon the previous one, similar to the Mayan step pyramids. Within these cycles were seven periods of light, called days, and six periods of dark, called nights. During the days, more light and information were taken in. The nights were time to rest, renew, and apply the information we had taken in during the day.

As humanity ascended the steps of the pyramid of consciousness that this calendar represented, the focus of consciousness expanded. The foun-

FIGURE 1: Mayan Step Pyramid at Chichen Itza, *(Photo courtesy of Bjorn Christian Torrissen, bjornfree.com/galleries.html).*

dational level or first cycle of the calendar was the cellular level. The next level was mammalian, then familial, tribal, cultural, national, planetary, galactic, and finally universal. Think of it as though you were looking through a microscope with a very small focal distance to begin. As you increased your focal distance or expanded your field of view, you saw that you are more than a collection of individual cells, more than an organism, or part of a family unit, etc. We carry the history of the expanded awareness of our ancestors in our DNA.

The last cycle of this calendar, the Universal Cycle, was characterized by conscious co-creation (Lungold 2005). The changes associated with this momentous time will continue for years past the 2012 end date, making this the perfect time for *Hardwired to Heaven!*

As human consciousness continues to shift in this next calendar, humanity, through the experience of increased energy from the sun and our galactic center, Earth changes, governmental and societal changes, and personal change is realizing that:

- It is through cooperation that we create lasting structures.
- Each individual is an empowered sovereign entity unto him or herself.
- Freedom is part of our essential nature.
- Through living in community we find our common unity.
- We are all connected via a matrix of energy or unified field and part of everything.
- We actualize our multidimensional nature by accessing other planes of existence through clairvoyance, clairaudience, clairsentience, claircognizance, bi-location and more.
- We are powerful creators of our reality.
- Conscious co-creation is the enlightened state.
- Connecting through the heart is the key to creating.
- Our desires manifest quickly and easily.
- Through balancing the heart and mind we reconnect to the earth's intelligence.
- Science and mysticism blend to become divine science.
- Peace and bliss are our birthright.
- Love is the guiding principle.

We have reached the end of our proverbial diving board. Below us await the keys to the Universe. It is time to jump in!

Physics and metaphysics are no longer separate. What was once thought of as *extra*sensory, *para*normal, *epi*phenomenal, or *extra*ordinary is easily explained by science. From the point of view of the unity, nothing is "extra" or "epi" – outside or above us. It all comes through us and from us – from our hearts, our means of connection with heaven. When we follow our hearts, we follow the pathways our hearts mapped for us. We download our divinity. Wouldn't it be nice to have a companion on this journey of awakening?

Here it is… from my heart.

CHAPTER TWO

A 'Hole' New World

*The thread of consciousness is woven into
the fabric of all matter. It is through this 'internet'
that divine intelligence orchestrates the cosmos.*

— *CYCLOPEA*

Physics and Metaphysics of Consciousness

Everything is made of energy. It is the stuff of what is. Where did the "stuff" come from? Good question. Scientists are still debating it. If the Universe started with a "big bang" (interesting that we use that word as slang for the procreative act!) where did the bang come from? What essentially went bang? Was it particles of energy, waves of light, strings of energy, or membranes? Membranes?!

One of the latest theories being tossed around the quantum mechanical world is the eleven-dimensional M-Theory. This hypothesizes that the multiverse (all that is) is made up of infinite universes. The number eleven refers to the number of space-time dimensions instead of the way we have been looking at the Universe, three dimensionally with a fourth dimension of time. Each universe is like a very thin membrane, 10^{-20} millimeters thick. These membrane universes are rippled and undulate like waves. Think of each membrane as a piece of super-thin ribbon candy that is still warm and able to move. Based on this theory, quantum physicists think our Universe was formed by the collision of two membrane universes. Was that what went bang?

According to another researcher, Nassim Haramein, we don't need quantum mechanics to explain the Universe. He used classical mechanical physics equations to show that what he believes created the Universe is the explosion of a black hole. His theory is based on the premise that at the center of the Universe and every part of the Universe is a black hole. After all, even quantum physicists agree that 99.999 percent of an atom is space. The Universe continues to expand and matter is continuously being created. Haramein believes the Universe must also contract to follow the axiom "for every action there is an equal and opposite reaction." Matter, according to Haramein, is what "leaks out of" the event horizon of the great black hole (Haramein 2010). (An event horizon is the portion of a black hole where gravity is so strong that nothing near it can escape. It's like getting too close to a huge whirlpool and getting sucked down into it.) If that's true, where did the first black hole come from?

Perhaps energy has always been around. After all, the law of conservation of energy states that energy can neither be created nor destroyed; it merely changes form. Form is an important word that we will revisit here from time to time.

Okay, so you have always been around since you are energy. Some may argue that this statement isn't true because they only identify with their mortal physical self and its limited lifespan. Once you recognize that you are not your physical body but a spiritual or energetic being that temporarily occupies a physical body, you realize that, like all energy, you are eternal. Good, let's move on.

Energy takes various forms such as chemical, mechanical, potential, kinetic, elastomeric, gravitational, thermal, electrical, magnetic, electromagnetic, nuclear, light, and sound. The human body carries out chemical reactions, conducts electricity, generates heat, creates electromagnetic fields, produces sound, and emits light through its chakras and aura. Quite an invention, isn't it? The human body is even more marvelous when you realize that all of these forms of energy are constantly changing and interacting in a very controlled manner. There is a very small margin of error for most of the functions of the human body. For example, the body can only function well in a very small blood pH range of 7.35 to 7.45. A blood pH of 6.8 can induce coma and even cause death.

So who or what is orchestrating the gazillion chemical reactions per minute conducted by the community of approximately 100 trillion cells that comprise your body? Are "you," your conscious awareness, choreographing an unfathomable number of chemical reactions per minute? There is no way our current conscious mind can take in and control this enormity of data. How, then, does each of your cells know what to do and how to do it amidst its trillions of neighbors and in a way that maintains homeostasis or an internal equilibrium? How do we maintain balance in a seeming sea of chaos?

The autonomic nervous system is responsible for maintaining our bodily functions such as heart rate, respiration, digestion, and elimination, and for our fight or flight responses. This system was mostly designed to run without conscious thought. I say mostly because we can consciously affect some of these functions like respiration. We are able to consciously take a breath or hold our breath.

Wonderful. So the autonomic nervous system choreographs the complex visceral internal workings of the body. I think by now you know my next question. Who or what made the autonomic nervous system? What intelligence thought up such an intricate system with built-in checks and balances that runs on autopilot for the most part? How do the cells that make up the autonomic nervous system know what to do?

It may sound like I am arguing for the existence of "God" or whatever term you prefer to use to describe this super intelligence. Yes and a bit more. If everything is made of energy, then this intelligence **is** energy.

One definition of intelligence is the gathering or distribution of information. In-*form*-ation. There is that word "form" again. The point I am really making is that energy, the stuff of what is, holds, carries, transmits, and is synonymous with, information. They are an inseparable team, a dynamic duo.

It is easy to understand how sound, electricity, light, and chemical energy transfer information. Our neurons or brain cells communicate with one another by using chemical energy in the synapses or spaces between the cells and electrical energy along the axon of the cell (see figure 2). We send messages through sound each time we speak. Within the dendrites and neurons of our nervous system – within most cells, for that matter – are tiny hollow hexagonal thread-like protein filaments called microtubules. These microtubules form the "spine" of the cell.

Dr. Stuart Hameroff, an anesthesiologist and leading researcher in human consciousness, suggests that microtubules act like conduit for light (information) to travel throughout the body (Hameroff 1987, 174 and McTaggart 2002, 92). I believe it is actually the water within the microtu-

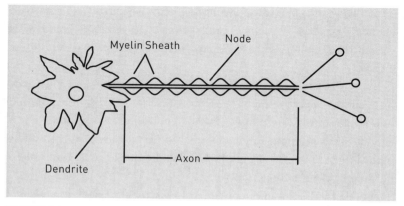

FIGURE 2: Neuron or Nerve Cell

bules that allows for the transference of information in the body. I will share more about the importance of water in Chapter 5, Blood and Water.

So, one possible definition of information we could use is "that part of energy that provides data to which a consciousness can respond." Here's the next question: What is consciousness?

We consider ourselves to be conscious beings. We are aware of our environment and have the ability to sense stimuli and respond. We can even be aware of our awareness and interact with ourselves. If we are energy, and intelligence flows with energy, then consciousness is also intelligence. Consciousness is self-aware, self-referring, and intelligent.

Unified Field

It seems that some quantum physicists are in agreement with my argument. The unified field theory postulates that at the most fundamental level of everything in the Universe is a unified field of energy. This unified field is the source of all energy, matter, and life. It is the substructure of the Universe and permeates everything. In fact, the unified field is fundamental intelligence and fundamental consciousness.

It is important to keep in mind that the unified field is multi-dimensional and does not look like a two-dimensional piece of graph paper. Rather, the field is a spiraling grid that resembles a donut.

Even Haramein agrees. He says that the vacuum, which is produced by the black hole, isn't empty but contains super-concentrated energy. This energy spirals in a vortex-like motion, contracts to the center point of super concentrated energy, stops for a nanosecond, changes direction, then spirals back out into the self-reflexive shape of the black hole, or torus. (The unified field is also called the vacuum and the zero-point energy field. Zero-point energy refers to that point of super concentrated energy.)

According to Haramein, the electromagnetic field and the gravitational field within this black hole are what feed back on each other to produce consciousness. He uses the term the "black-white whole" to describe the Universe. Since consciousness is self-aware there must be a feedback mechanism. The energy from the vacuum (the field) informs matter and the energy of matter informs the vacuum in a never-ending game of information ping-pong. As we feed information into the vacuum, the vacuum integrates it and feeds it back to us (Haramein 2010).

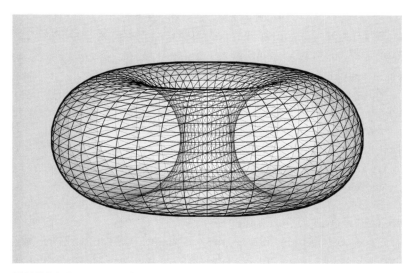

FIGURE 3: Torus Spiral Grid

Consciousness is a form of information. Matter is the "form" and Spirit is the "in" or inspiration of in-form-ation. Since consciousness is a form of information, and all energy carries information, then all energy is consciousness. From this perspective, Einstein's Relativity Equation, $E=MC^2$, equates to Consciousness (or energy E) = Matter (or mass M) multiplied by Light/Spirit (C) squared.

Consciousness is a product of matter and light. Hence, consciousness must have a physical form or mass, whether that form is a sacred geometric structure of energy, a rock, a tree, or a human being, to be conscious of itself. The only way God or the unified field knows itself is through informing itself, being in form and informing the form. In addition, this equation suggests that if we increase the amount of light we receive (from the sun and galactic center), our consciousness increases at a much faster rate than if we merely increase our mass.

We live in a holographic Universe, which means that every level of creation is mirrored in each part or fractal. No wonder the ancient Greeks inscribed this sentence in the Temple of Delphi: *"Know yourself and you will know the Universe and the Gods."* If I study and understand the workings of the human body, I will understand the workings of the Universe.

Human Consciousness

A group of five researchers, Jibu, Hagan, Hameroff, Pribram, and Yasue, decided to collaborate on human intelligence and came up with the following theory of human consciousness.

Microtubules within our cells are the means through which information, in the form of light, travels through the body. This propagation or movement of information is dependent upon the coherent resonance of these structures. Once these microtubules vibrate in phase with one another so that their wave formations are similar and in harmony (coherence) they create a global coherence of waves called superradiance. Superradiance is the product of carefully arranged water molecules and the quantum electromagnetic field inside microtubules.

Information, in the form of photons (light), travels instantaneously throughout the "information scaffold" or cytoskeleton of cells, which is partially comprised of microtubules (Jibu et al. 1994, 199). Our cells, the basic building blocks of our bodies, are like a symphony of tiny individual vibrating tuning forks that orchestrates the unfathomable number of chemical reactions, electrical impulses, mechanical movements, etc., that occur every second of our life. We'll come back to this later, but remember that water is always a part of each of these reactions, impulses and movements. More importantly, light is the maestro of this symphony and, thus, of the body.

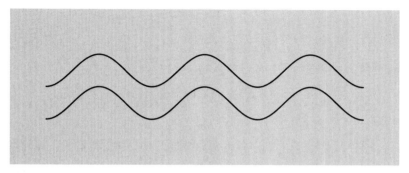

FIGURE 4: Wave Coherence

The theoretical biophysicist Fritz-Albert Popp found through his research that biophotons (light) are given off within and between body cells with a high degree of coherence (Popp, Gu, and Li 1994, 1293). Biophotons or light can act like a wave and coherent biophotons exhibit harmonic wave function (see figure 4). He also discovered that cells and organisms can intelligently communicate through these coherent light emissions (Popp, Gu, and Li 1994, 1270). Lynne McTaggart writes in her book, *The Field: The Quest for the Secret Force of the Universe*, that Popp surmised that fundamental consciousness is coherent light and that consciousness is not limited to the brain but exists throughout the body (McTaggart 2002, 94).

Could this unified zero-point energy field or vacuum be synonymous with God? Is it the field that informs the light? Yes, and more specifically, it is the *heart* of the field.

Current Human Consciousness

Until recently, human consciousness perceived a dualistic reality: up-down, light-dark, right-wrong, on-off. As our consciousness evolves, our perception of the Universe changes. What we had perceived to be opposites, exclusive in nature, and separate, quantum physics now insists is otherwise. Phrases such as "quantum phase entanglements" and "nonlocal connections" describe how intimately the particles/waves/strings of what is are connected. In fact, the unified field theory includes a nonlocal reality, one in which a particle can influence a distant particle instantaneously, faster than the speed of light, without anything passing between them. In addition, when two particles interact and affect each other, they are said to be entangled.

We are all connected by the unified field that flows through us, thereby interacting with the field and everything in it. We are all entangled within this matrix of energy. How could it be otherwise if at the basis of everything in the Universe is a *unified* field? The mystics have known for centuries that we are all connected.

When we replace dualism with unity, our consciousness takes one giant step forward. We finally see that everything is connected, but only when we look through our hearts and not with our minds. Here we can experience unconditional love, which naturally flows when we awaken to unity consciousness.

Things still appear black or white when we come from a place of unity. What changes is our perception that black means the absence of white. We are now able to entertain the notion that white can exist within black and that the two are not mutually exclusive. This notion is expressed in the Chinese yin yang Taijitu symbol. What seem to be opposites are actually complementary, interconnected, and interdependent. In fact, the Universe could not exist without the polar opposites of positive and negative charge. It is because of these opposites, or any opposites, that the Universe can create anything.

Nothing in the Universe is entirely black or entirely white. Even black holes are not all black. In fact, for every black hole, there must be a sun

FIGURE 5: Chinese Taijitu Symbol

since the Universe operates through opposites. The center black hole of the torus-shaped unified field has as its opposite the Great Central Sun. Together they form the container for an unknown number of holographic multiverses or black-white wholes. This model of the Universe fits with Jesus' words from the King James Bible (John 14:2): "In my Father's house are many mansions." There is one unifying container (the Universe) that holds a myriad of multiverses.

It is important to keep in mind that as our consciousness increases, we break the plane of existence from one dimension to another. When we do this, we enter a new spiral matrix at that dimension. Consciousness, like everything else in the Universe, has its own grid within the master grid. The form of our consciousness grid changes as our consciousness increases since it is form or shape that informs. The form changes from one platonic solid to another.

Remember the five platonic solids from high school geometry? If you don't, they are the tetrahedron, cube, octahedron, icosahedron, and dodecahedron, shown from left to right in figure 6 below, starting with tetrahedron. The Christ consciousness grid is shaped like a stellated dodecahedron

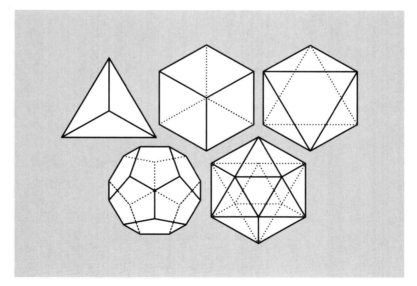

FIGURE 6: The Platonic Solids

31

FIGURE 7: Stellated Dodecahedron

(figure 7). We are all ascending into this consciousness grid. Remember, there is no consciousness without in-*form*-ation. Sacred geometry is the blueprint of the cosmos. All that is comes from these forms.

When we change our consciousness grid, we change our perspective and see the world through different eyes. We are looking through the lens of higher dimensional awareness.

When we awaken to the truth that we are part of this unified field, that we are in the field and the field is within us, we become nonlocal, meaning we bi-locate, we remote-view, and we open psychically to our original divine nature. We were designed to be clairvoyant, clairaudient, clairsentient, and claircognizant, just as Jesus and other masters were.

Through centuries of control and dumbing us down by those in power, we have forgotten our connection to heaven. We have come to believe that we are not powerful enough to do these things. We have been told it was a sin, it was against the law, or we would go to hell. As a result, we created our own hell on earth. Now it is time to co-create our heaven on earth.

CHAPTER THREE

A Creative Energy Story

You are but one of a multitude of heavenly hosts, angels,
call it what you will. Your idea of heaven is outside of yourself.
I am here to tell you it is within. You are the angels, the heavenly
ones who are part of the heavens...the energy of creation.

— CYCLOPEA

In the beginning, the number 3 was inscribed on the breath of the deity. When the deity spoke, all of creation listened. Prime Creator, being whole unto itself, allowed the energy of what is to follow these decrees:

1. The energy shall differentiate into masculine and feminine, the initiatory and the receptive, the electro and the magnetic, and shall also be known as positive (proton) and negative (electron).
2. All matter shall be made of these qualities.
3. Opposites shall have an affinity for each other.
4. Similar frequencies of vibration attract.
5. These affinities and attractions are the prime movers of all matter.
6. All matter tends toward the state of neutrality (neutrons), a dynamic balance of charges, and returns to Source or Spirit, the formless state of the consciousness of Prime Creator.

The energy of creation heeded the call. Negative charge began to move in a wave pattern, forming crests and troughs. Positive charge produced an identical wave pattern. The charges began to dance as they approached each other, coming together and moving apart in harmony with each other's rhythm. The electro and magnetic, the masculine and feminine joined in the dance. The energies weaved in and out, up and down until the pattern of movement was embedded in the matrix.

As the polarities of creative energy flowed toward each other and then apart, they created crests and troughs, high points and low points. These turning points or nodes formed along the common axis of these waves where the two waves crossed. The nodes became tiny zero-point fields where the opposites were joined and the charges were neutralized. Thus the holographic zero-point energy field mirrored itself in each node. Creation used these nodes or turning points as a means to expedite the flow of energy. The energy could jump from node to node instead of traversing the entire wave. Hence, dolphins would swim and woodpeckers would fly following these waves, and nerve impulses would follow the nodes of the myelin sheath along the axon of nerve cells (see figure 2) to speed the flow of information. These waves move in a pattern called sine waves.

The masculine and the feminine were joined, the mother giving birth to matter. From that moment on, all creation would follow this form. DNA, a recorder of information, would follow this double helix pattern, again exemplifying the holographic nature of the Universe.

From this prime triangle or holy trinity, the energy moved in formation and produced all other forms. The form itself became in**form**ation. The light took on form and it was through form that consciousness would communicate.

Once matter and light began to dance, moving up and down, in and out, a strange thing occurred: Matter and light began to move in a circular fashion causing the entire pattern to rotate. This corkscrew motion of the

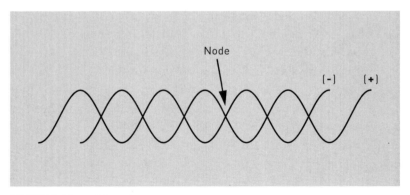

FIGURE 8: Flow of Creation

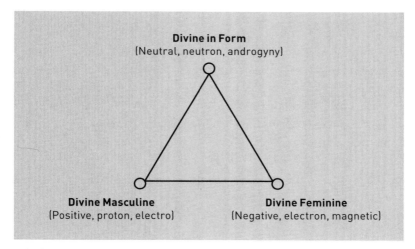

Divine in Form
(Neutral, neutron, androgyny)

Divine Masculine
(Positive, proton, electro)

Divine Feminine
(Negative, electron, magnetic)

FIGURE 9: Prime Triangle

two rotating sine waves where light and matter spin around a common axis produced orbital angular momentum. As the momentum began to build, a being was spun into existence. All conscious beings would be formed from this blending of light or Spirit and matter. It would also be from this spiraling caduceus energy that spin would originate.

The sine wave became the harmonic expression of Source energy. Source flowed following this pattern. Just as Source energy is infinite, the movement of two sine waves, 180 degrees out of phase (opposite

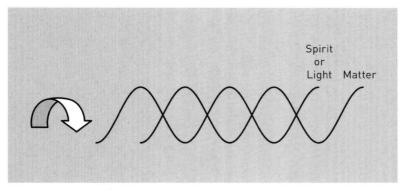

Spirit
or
Light   Matter

FIGURE 10: Spiraling Caduceus of Light and Matter

movement from each other), formed the symbol for infinity, ∞. This mirroring of two identical sine waves across a common axis canceled out any charge, leaving the entire system neutral, balanced, and in harmony. Every system in nature would seek to attain this balance. It would be from precisely this vortex-like movement that the zero-point energy field or unified field would be created.

As protons and electrons moved in a spiraling pattern, they created a web of consciousness. This type of movement and spin produced a torus. (The Universe is shaped like a doughnut or a torus, spiraling out and then coming back into the center to begin a different cycle. The torus shape naturally confers the self-reflexive nature of consciousness. The unified field or zero-point energy field is represented by this pattern, which originated from the Flower of Life or the master pattern of the Universe.)

Within the blessed trinity of the prime triangle the divine spiraling movement of creation emerged. It is the Golden Mean Spiral or Phi ratio, the sacred proportion (see figure 14).

All of creation followed this divine proportion, creating nothing but beauty. It dictated how the material world would take form. Since all of creation would be birthed according to this proportion, it would become the expression of love. (Within the unified field of the torus is this spiraling of creation. Love is the primal creative force of the Universe.)

When opposites came together, when female and male merged, creative

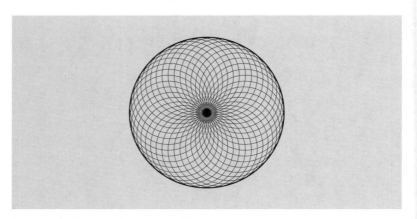

FIGURE 11: Torus as Viewed from Above

FIGURE 12: Flower of Life

energy was produced. Similarly, when a woman or man balanced the masculine and feminine energies within, she or he became like the deity and was capable of creation. This merging of masculine and feminine energies took the form of two prime triangles in perfect balance inscribed within the circle, the totality. All of creation was formed through this division of the space. The balance of opposites was the foundation for the whole of creation.

(Haramein also believes that space divides itself by the form of a star tetrahedron inscribed in a circle (Haramein 2010).)

FIGURE 13: Two Prime Triangles (Star Tetrahedron) Inscribed Within a Circle

CHAPTER FOUR

The Heart of Matter

*In your heart, time and space do not exist for your heart
is always connected to the cosmic heart. The heart of
every particle of matter remembers its divinity.*

— *CYCLOPEA*

When I was researching sayings or phrases pertaining to parts of the body, I discovered that, by far, the body part linked with the most sayings is the heart. I bet you can think of at least ten sayings right off the top of your head. Here are just a few of the ones I found:

Offer one's heart
Take something to heart
Do something by heart
From the bottom of one's heart
At the heart of something
The heart of the matter
Heart of hearts
Heart and soul
Eat one's heart out
Break one's heart
Have a heart
Change of heart
Have the heart to
Lose heart
Wear one's heart on one's sleeve
With all one's heart
Wholeheartedly
Heart of gold

Out of the goodness of one's heart
Home is where the heart is
You're all heart
Cross my heart.

Why do we have so much fascination with the heart? Why is the heart so important to us? Every great spiritual master and religion teaches the importance of the heart. Sufism is known as the religion of the heart, and Christianity speaks of the sacred heart of Jesus. If you were the Prime Creator, what would you choose as your heart?

The Heart of Creation

What is at the heart of creation? The Maya believe that there is a place at the center of our galaxy where all consciousness or energy originates. This place is actually the black hole in the center of the Milky Way. Scientists have found black holes at the center or "at the heart" of all galaxies. This certainly supports Haramein's model of the Universe described on page 23. Black holes can be the result of stars going supernova. A supernova event may be triggered because the core of an ageing large star stops producing energy from nuclear fusion and undergoes gravitational collapse. In other words, it falls in on itself creating a hole which continues to pull in surrounding energy.

If the Law of Conservation of Energy is still true, then the enormous amount of energy swallowed by these alleged voids must go somewhere. It does. Energy goes in, and astrophysicists believe it comes out through quasars that are powered by black holes. Quasars are believed to be the most powerful objects in the Universe. Science*Daily* reported on July 24, 2013 that astrophysicists Hainline, Hickox, Greene, Myers, and Zakamska discovered that quasars emit full spectrum radiation (light) through their galaxy.

The amount of energy produced by these quasars is estimated to be a thousand times that of all the stars in our Milky Way galaxy (Dartmouth College 2013). In addition, NASA has found that the jets from black holes redistribute matter and energy (NASA 2006). Thus, black holes and quasars are the great recyclers in the sky.

Artists' renditions of black holes (NASA's images of black holes only show a two-dimensional image of the spiral of stars around the center black hole of a galaxy) depict them shaped like, you guessed it, a torus! According to the Haramein-Rauscher dual torus structure of black holes, black holes take in material/information *and* radiate it out in the form of electromagnetic radiation (Haramein 2010). According to the Haramein-Rauscher theory, the two holes have a dual structure and function that, as I pointed out in Chapter 2, Haramein calls the black-white whole. I like this term since it suggests that opposites exist at every level and form of creation.

Haramein believes that spin produces polarization (Haramein 2010). Perhaps the origin of spin comes from the infinite spiral dance of positive and negative charges (polar opposites) as mentioned in Chapter 3. Since everything is made of these charges, this spin continues in all of nature. Of course, this is just my spin on things! Maybe it is just another version of the age-old question, "Which came first, the chicken or the egg?" In this case, did spin produce polarization or did polar opposites produce spin? Now my head is spinning!

At the center of the great black hole is an infinitesimally small, super-concentrated point of energy – absolute zero point, the nothingness from which all energy originates. It is within this point that all motion and still-ness is held, where no energy and all energy exist simultaneously. It is filled with every possible creation and at the same time, empty. This is the great mystery: opposites must exist simultaneously for creation to occur.

It is the in-breath and out-breath of the Universe or the expansion and contraction as Haramein refers to it. The zero-point energy field, which at the same time holds the minimum amount of energy a system can hold and surpasses all physical energy by a factor of 10^{40}, is made of a multitude of black holes surrounding the center point. Each point on the grid is a mini black hole, a mini zero-point. Every level of creation mirrors this, including your heart and going all the way down to the atomic level.

At the heart of matter, then, is a black hole or zero point. Every atom, every cell, every galaxy has a black hole. At the same time, its opposite must exist. So paired with each black hole is a quasar or sun. What is true of one part of the Universe must be true for all other parts since the Universe is fractal or holographic. Thus, the hermetic axiom, "As above so below, as within so without" fully and simply explains the nature of the Universe.

Everything has a polar opposite, even black holes. Their polar opposite is a sun. Your heart contains the master black hole and your sun for your body. Remember all of those paintings of the Sacred Heart of Jesus and Jesus pointing to his heart, which had flames and gold coming from it? That is your sun and your light.

The Human Heart

When you were conceived, the first thing your unique golden-mean vortex of energy did was spin your heart into physical form: The heart is the first organ or tissue to form. That's right. At one point in your development, you were "all heart." This vortex energy is the same energy that spins in the great void, the source of everything. Your heart, and the rest of your body, is shaped from this spinning energy.

If you look at its shape closely, you will see an apex or lower point of the heart and you will see, also, that the top of the heart is considerably larger than the apex. Vortex energy looks like a tornado, shaped like a cone. The heart has a slightly distorted conical shape. This distortion comes from the mingling of human and divine energies, or light and matter. The rate at which light is stepped down in frequency into physical form varies depending on each person's original divine blueprint.

Theodor Schwenk reminds us in *Sensitive Chaos: The Creation of Flowing Forms in Water and Air* that our bodies originated mostly from water and that it is the flow of water that dictates our resultant physical form. He goes on to say that the heart's fibers were spun out of the same vortex-like motion that water so eloquently exemplifies, thus producing that same motion in the blood that the heart pumps (Schwenk 2008, 91-92).

As seen in an MRI of the heart, the fibers of the surface epicardial layer spiral clockwise and the fibers of the subendocardial layer spiral counterclockwise and all three layers of the heart twist forming a vortex at its apex (Buckberg et al. 2008, 2574-75). The spiral shape of the fibers of the heart and its overall vortex shape help to spin the blood through the vessels. The layers of muscle spiral around each other, following the golden-mean ratio. Since the heart is shaped like a vortex, it naturally produces the Golden Mean.

The Golden Mean or Phi ratio is found throughout nature. It is defined by segmenting a line into two sections, one larger than the other. The ratio of the sum of these segments to the larger segment is equal to the ratio of the larger segment to the smaller one. This ratio is an irrational number

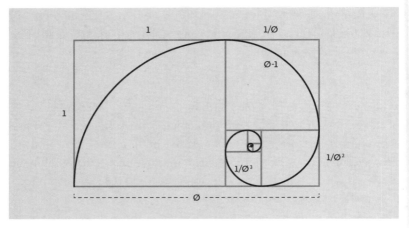

FIGURE 14: Golden Mean Spiral

approximating 1.6180339887... that is mirrored in the human body. For example, the ratio of the length of the forearm to the length of the hand is the golden-mean ratio or divine proportion.

Figure 15, below, is an artist's rendition of a positively charged "male" atom and a negatively charged "female" atom as first depicted in *Occult Chemistry* by Annie Besant and Charles W. Leadbeater. The book was pub-

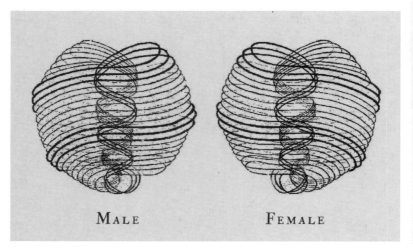

FIGURE 15: Male and Female Atom Depictions Shaped Like a Heart *(Taken from Occult Chemistry: Clairvoyant Observations on the Chemical Elements)*

lished in 1919, but Leadbeater first intuited this depiction in 1895 (Besant and Leadbeater 1919). Note that the overall shape of each is like that of a human heart and that their inner vortex spirals (each with a different direction of spin) look like the caduceus sine wave in the previous chapter! These spirals naturally form the golden mean which is also found in egg shapes. I included these drawings since they are an eloquent visual for what the spiraling energies look like inside and surrounding the heart.

Each human organ has a unique tone or set of parameters that determine its shape. Sound and form are interchangeable determinants. A wonderful example of this has been documented by crop circle researchers who have recorded sounds coming from inside these sacred geometry imprints. Similarly, cymatics, the study of the inherent geometries within sound, shows how sound creates form.

Your heart's tone is the same as the sound from the core of the central or "great" black-white whole, only with its volume turned down. As I wrote in *In the Key of Life*, "At the heart of who you are is a love song that has always been resonating" (Cerio 2007, 28). This song is the harmonic expression of the golden-mean spiral.

The Heart through a Different Mind

Until now, we have looked at our world through a three-dimensional mind. As our consciousness expands, the way we see our world expands with it. We are now starting to see with a fourth-dimensional lens; soon we will view it through a fifth-dimensional lens. Think of it as changing the focal length of a microscope. You will see things in the field of view that weren't there at a different focal length. When we realize that every cell has its own consciousness, we change our view of the human body. It is no longer a mass of bones, organs, and muscle, but a living community of conscious beings.

Science once believed that the heart's primary function was to pump blood throughout the body. Recent scientific research, though, has opened the door to more unconventional and expansive views of the function of the human heart.

The heart, for example, is a key player in maintaining homeostasis or a stable internal environment. The notion that the only function of the heart is to pump is antiquated. According to a paper published in a December

1984 supplement to the Journal of the International Society of Hypertension, a group of researchers concluded that the heart is an endocrine gland that integrates cardiovascular homeostasis, meaning it helps to regulate hormones, nutrients, and waste products in the blood (Cantin et al. 1984, 329). According to a February 25, 2008 American Physiological Society press release, the hormone, atrial natriuretic factor or ANF, was discovered by Aldolfo deBold in 1981. He named it "atrial" because it is produced in the atrium of the heart and "natriuretic" because it helps the body remove excess sodium through the urine.

The press release also relayed that Dr. David Vesely, a professor at USF, later discovered three more hormones that open the blood vessels, lower blood pressure and increase potassium excretion, and another that functions similarly to the atrial natriuretic factor that deBold found. Vesely found that these same heart hormones cured pancreatic cancer and breast cancer in the majority of the mice treated (American Physiological Society 2008).

Clearly, the heart controls more than the movement of fluid.

Another way the heart regulates homeostasis is by monitoring the blood. The heart is in constant communication with the rest of the body by assessing the blood that flows through it. We'll learn more about the importance of blood and the heart in the next chapter.

Neuroscientists recently discovered a whole network of brain tissue (neurons) within the human heart, triggering a new field of medicine called neurocardiology. The heart produces the neurotransmitters dopamine, norepinephrine, and acetylcholine, special chemicals that transmit informational signals from a neuron to a cell (Buhner 2004, 81). The heart, like the brain, is in constant contact with the rest of the body, not only neurologically, but biochemically through neurotransmitters and hormones. Feeling does originate in the heart.

The Heart's Electromagnetic Field

The similarities between your heart and the unified field do not end there. Not only is your heart shaped like a vortex, the shape of the electromagnetic field it produces mirrors that of the Universe. Remember that the Universe is shaped like a donut or torus. The electromagnetic field around your heart is also shaped like a torus. Even the red blood cells pumped by the heart are shaped like a torus. In addition, the earth's electromagnetic field is shaped like a torus and our heart's field is connected to the earth's field, which is connected to the Universe. If you move the "h" and put it in front of the "e" in the word earth, it spells the word heart. Each red blood cell generates its own mini electromagnetic field created by the iron in its hemoglobin (I'll talk more about hemoglobin in Chapters 5 and 6, the negative charge on the surface of the cell, and its toroidal shape). Each of these small magnetic fields combines to form a larger field – that of the heart.

As such, blood facilitates the movement of electromagnetic waves (Buhner 2004, 86). The combination of electrical impulses generated within the heart and the magnetic blood flowing through it produces the strongest electromagnetic field of the human body.

The heart's electric field is 60 times stronger and its magnetic field is 5,000 times stronger than the brain's (McCraty, Bradley, and Tomasino 2004-5, 16). In fact, the Institute for HeartMath˙ has demonstrated that brain waves harmonize to the heart's waves (McCraty, Atkinson, and Tomasino 2001). Additionally, the Institute for HeartMath˙ found evidence that the heart receives intuitive information before the brain (McCraty, Bradley, and Tomasino 2004-5, 17).

It is the heart, not the brain that is really running the show. Think of your heart as mission control and the brain as flight crew. Mission control

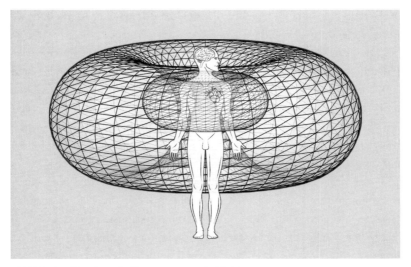

FIGURE 16: The Heart's Electromagnetic Field

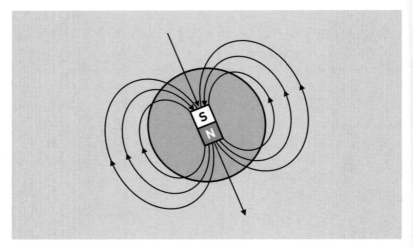

FIGURE 17: The Earth's Electromagnetic Field

maps the journey. It looks at incoming data to make course corrections and then notifies the flight crew of the changes. The flight crew plugs in the new coordinates and assesses the situation. This information is transmitted to mission control and then the final decision is made based on all the data. When heart and brain work together and the brain waves harmonize to the heart waves and not vice versa, we shift our focus from head-centered to heart-centered. When we are heart-centered, our mental chatter quiets, we make better decisions, and we become more intuitive.

The heart's main purpose is to orchestrate the soul in human form. Each of us embodies with a soul mission. The heart's electromagnetic field is in constant communication with the unified field, your original divine blueprint, and your template for this incarnation. It is sending and receiving signals to and from your soul to guide you in this life. This is how the heart creates the path you follow and why we intuitively know to follow our hearts.

The orchestration of your life is multi-dimensional. From molecule to cell to organ to organism to human intelligence to cosmic consciousness, your heart is your connection to the divine consciousness, your essential self. When you live through your heart, you follow your hardwired connection to the intelligence of the Universe and to the heart of matter.

CHAPTER FIVE

Blood and Water

Blood is an elixir from heaven,
an alchemical mixture of water and light.

— *CYCLOPEA*

What do blood and water have to do with using the heart for creating, you ask? Both are essential for life and, as you will soon read, carry more than needed nutrients and chemicals.

Blood

Blood is symbolic of life and mortality. How can we forget the scene in the movie *Dances with Wolves* when Kevin Costner reluctantly accepts the offer from his Sioux friend to drink the blood from the liver of a freshly killed buffalo? Native Americans knew of the life-giving energy contained within the blood.

Blood was and is still used by some in various rituals as an offering or sacrifice to atone for sins, to purify, or to sanctify. The Aztecs, Incas, and Israelites performed blood sacrifices to keep their gods happy – the Aztecs to keep the sun moving and the Israelites to keep the covenant of God with his people. The Aztecs believed the life-giving spirit is in the blood and concentrates in the heart.

The term "heart-blood" refers to the blood within the chambers of the heart and not the blood within the vessels. This heart-blood is precious life essence and is often interpreted as essential to one's happiness. What makes blood so magical, mystical, and life-giving?

Blood is a heterogeneous solution that moves through living things. Its main purpose is to transport oxygen, nutrients, disease-fighting cells, hormones, proteins, etc. In other words, it is the substrate of the body's transport system. The yellow substrate within the blood is called plasma.

When all of the cells, hormones, dissolved gases and proteins are removed from the blood, what remains is water, which constitutes 90 percent of its volume.

Another definition of plasma is the fourth state of matter, the other three being solid, liquid, and gas. Plasma is ionized gas; gas that is so energized that it frees its electrons. It was named after blood plasma by Nobel Laureate, Irving Langmuir. Langmuir looked at blood plasma as a sea of conducting ions, such as sodium and potassium. Since the ionized gas clouds he observed seemed to intelligently organize when electrical currents or magnetic fields were introduced, he likened them to blood plasma. Our sun is a huge ball of plasma that appears yellow to us, just like our blood plasma. However, blood plasma is mainly water.

In utero, the mother's blood is essential to provide needed nutrition, proteins, oxygen, etc., for the healthy development of the fetus. As mentioned in Chapter 4, the heart is the first organ to form, since the blood must circulate throughout the fetus to keep it alive. Ancient Egyptians believed that the metaphysical heart was formed from one drop of the mother's blood at the time of conception. In addition to blood, water in the womb provides the ideal environment for growth and protection.

We know that blood and water are essential for human life. J. J. Hurtak also wrote about the significance of blood and water in, *The Book of Knowledge: The Keys of Enoch* (Key 115: 45-47): Blood, water and Spirit are the vehicles through which life enters our body. Blood makes us sacred and through water we uphold the will of God (Hurtak, 1987, 145).

FIGURE 18: Red Blood Cell

In ancient times, wine was mixed with water to purify the water and make it taste better. In Catholicism, water and wine are symbolic of Christ's blood. The Catholic Church usually uses red wine, the red color symbolizing blood, or more specifically the red blood cells that carry oxygen.

Remember that red blood cells are torus-shaped, like the Universe. They are the microcosm of the universal intelligence within the body. Everywhere within life, the divine is replicated and evidenced. The unified field literally flows through us. Just as the iron core of Earth is integral to Earth's electromagnetic field, each red blood cell has iron in its hemoglobin. The breath of God, oxygen or prana, runs through our blood, carried within the hemoglobin molecule.

Water, one could argue, represents the plasma portion of blood. During Catholic Mass, the water and wine are mixed while the priest may say, "By the mystery of this water and wine may we come to *share in the divinity* [author's emphasis] of Christ who humbled himself to share in our humanity." Once the water and wine are mixed, they cannot be separated. Once we download our divinity, we cannot go backwards in consciousness. It also serves to remind that there is no separation between God and human. Is there something special that happens within our blood and water that makes us divine?

Perhaps this is why Jesus said his time had not come yet when his mother asked him to take care of the shortage of wine at the wedding in Cana. He knew that once he literally changed water into wine, he would symbolically change his life from wise teacher to divine master. Once this news spread, he would never be seen in the same way again. He knew that all things come in divine time. So the question I have is, "Why did he perform the 'miracle' if it was not his time?"

Jesus supposedly fulfilled a prophecy about flowing wine and, at the same time, formed a new covenant. In the old covenant, blood, from a lamb without blemish, placed on the mercy seat of the Ark of the Covenant atoned for sins. The only time Jesus purportedly spoke the word "covenant" was at the Last Supper when he spoke of his blood as being the new covenant. To make an oath in blood is the most powerful and binding oath one can make.

When we speak about blood, we often use it to refer to being part of the same family, as through a bloodline. To make a covenant in blood is to infer we are all related by blood to Christ and to one another. We are all one family, one bloodline.

If Christ was a master, then so are we.

Water

Not only is water the most abundant compound on Earth, constituting 70 percent of the planet's surface, it is abundant throughout the Universe. In 2011, a large team of astronomers found one of the Universe's oldest, largest, and most distant watering holes: a black hole within a quasar galaxy, surrounded by 140 trillion times all the water in the earth's oceans! That's astronomical! This finding suggests that water may have been around since the time of the Big Bang (NASA 2011 and Bradford et al. 2011, 1).

Water is a unique molecule: It is the only common substance that can exist as a solid (ice), liquid, or gas (steam); and at certain temperatures, it can exist as all three at the same time! This is called a triple-point temperature.

As most substances will dissolve in water, it is called the universal solvent. Luckily, all the necessary components of blood dissolve in water, otherwise how would life transport them? Without water, we would not be able to regulate respiration, digestion, elimination, endocrine secretions, body temperature, and more.

The shape of the water molecule also makes it unique. It forms a distorted tetrahedron (four-sided figure) since there are two pairs of electrons on the oxygen atom repelling each other and therefore "pushing" down on

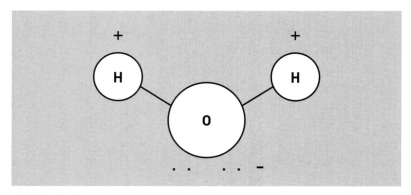

FIGURE 19: Water Molecule

the two hydrogen atoms, changing their angle from 109.5 (which is normally found in a tetrahedron) to 107.5 degrees. Each of these lone electron pairs along with the two hydrogen atoms form the legs of the tetrahedron with oxygen in the center.

Since oxygen is a much stronger electron hoarder than hydrogen, the oxygen end of the molecule is negatively charged and the hydrogen end is positively charged, creating a dipole moment. This polar property of water makes it a good conductor of electricity. The electrical dipole formed by water is extremely important to all life, especially as it relates to consciousness. Without it, we could not exist under standard temperatures and pressures. The dipole pulls water molecules tightly together, which raises its boiling point, or the temperature at which the liquid water becomes a gas. Life is grateful that water has a large liquid temperature range! Although we have a phrase, "It makes my blood boil," we all know that if our blood did boil we would die.

There is another property of water that keeps the boiling point high. As the molecules of water get closer, the hydrogen atoms of one water molecule, which are positively charged, are attracted to the negatively charged oxygen atom of another water molecule and form what is known as hydrogen bonds. It is these bonds, which are in a constant state of breaking and reforming as water molecules move, that aid in keeping the boiling point high. The hydrogen bond is what makes water uniquely qualified as life's substrate.

As we know, water will extinguish most fires. This is quite interesting when hydrogen by itself is flammable and oxygen by itself supports fire. So the elements that comprise water support another element, fire. Water is the amalgamation of fire and air. How awesome is it to take a flammable gas and combine it with a necessary component of fire in a unique way to produce a liquid that is not only non-flammable, but is essential for life. How about that for an alchemical process!

Hydrogen is the first and fundamental element of the Periodic Chart, having only one electron and one proton. It is a gas at standard temperature and pressure. The sun is comprised mainly of hydrogen, the lightest of all of the elements. It is interesting that the *lightest* element makes up stars, the largest bodies in the Universe. Did you catch the play on words again? Stars give off light. Our sun provides the light for our planet. So when you are told the key to enlightenment is to lighten up, believe it!

Oxygen is a heavier gas than hydrogen, comprising about 21 percent of the air we breathe. It is the most abundant element by mass within the earth, in her air, and in her seas, and the most abundant element by mass in the Universe. We need oxygen to carry out aerobic respiration so we can take food and turn it into usable energy. The ancients have known that the life force, the chi or prana, is taken in with the breath. The oxygen molecule, which partly comprises water, is innately intelligent. It is interesting that the most abundant chemical element on Earth uses the same symbol (O) as that of the number zero – zero-point energy.

As you will soon read in the next chapter, hemoglobin, which carries oxygen to the cells and takes carbon dioxide away from them, is comprised of four subunits. Guess what is in between these subunits, which is responsible for their intelligent structure? I'll give you a hint. This room temperature liquid is capable of forming hydrogen bonds. Yes, it's water!

Water is used in the sacrament of baptism, which is common in Christian traditions. The purpose of baptism is to cleanse the soul of original sin, which is necessary for salvation. In the Jewish tradition, the mikvah, a ritual immersion in water, is used as a purification rite, especially for women after menstruation or childbirth. Why is water deemed so important for these religious rites?

Perhaps the answer lies in water's structure when in solid form and in the ability of water to structure itself. The hexagonal structure of an ice crystal mirrors the fundamental shape of how space divides itself to create matter – a star tetrahedron. (More about the star tetrahedron in the following chapter, The Sacred Coordinate – God's USB Port.) The basic structure of the Universe informs water, which then in turn informs all life in our biosphere.

Structured water occurs when water molecules through hydrogen bonding form dipoles that facilitate the polarization of the overall structural layer of water (see figure 33). This structure, which accounts for water's liquid crystalline properties, facilitates the movement of electromagnetic radiation or light through the structure. Water transfers bits of light information just as the liquid crystal screen of your TV translates the light it receives into various colors and intensities.

Since water has dipole moments, it resonates at a similar frequency as microwaves. When polar ends line up within water creating a dipole moment, this allows the molecules to vibrate and "carry" the same frequency as the information. In other words, they come into resonance with the frequency of the electromagnetic radiation (light).

Water on the surface of the earth, within its oceans, seas, lakes, ponds, rivers, and streams, is exposed to light. Some of this light is refracted and enters the water and some is reflected. Think of water as a two-way door that swings in and out allowing light to enter or exit. Water acts as a transceiver of light, stair-stepping down its energy so that its information can be imprinted within the structure of water. This is one way new information gets imparted to all life, especially to marine life that does not have blood, such as hydra, sponges, coral, and blue-green algae.

According to Theodor Schwenk, water is the medium through which Earth and the cosmos communicates (Schwenk 2008, 68). Water, no matter where it is found in the Universe, is intelligently connected. Light informs water when it enters it, water informs the field, and the light/information that leaves the water has now been reformed or rewritten. The self-reflexive Universe is in constant communication with itself through the dance of light and water.

The unique property of structured water accounts for all of physical matter created by life forms. Without water's ability to structure itself and thereby become a superhighway of coherent information, our bodies would turn into a lifeless amorphous blob.

Blood, Water, and Enlightenment

The Hopi say that water is alive and intelligent. A well-known water researcher, Dr. Masaru Emoto, thinks he has successfully demonstrated that water has the ability to resonate with various forms of vibration, such as words or music. Emoto found that positive, uplifting words and sounds imparted into water – through writing the word on a container, saying or sending the word over a container, or playing music near a container of water – produce beautiful crystals when a small sample of that water is frozen. When water is imprinted with negative thoughts such as "I hate you," it does not produce those beautiful crystals: It produces an ugly, unrecognizable frozen drop of water (Emoto 2010). His work with water may demonstrate the intelligence of water to which the Hopi refer.

Jacques Benveniste was a much ridiculed researcher for his avant-garde notion that water can hold memory and that this ability is influenced by electromagnetic fields (Schiff 1995, 33). He first thought of the notion that water could act as a "template" for information while conducting an experiment in 1988 with twelve fellow researchers. Benveniste and his colleagues were surprised by their findings: A highly diluted solution with water still produced a similar effect as if the molecule (in this case, anti-immunoglobulin E) was still present (Davenas, E. et. al. 1988, 818).

From Emoto's and Benveniste's work, we can surmise that water holds memory or frequency, since our thoughts are energy. It stands to reason, then, given that we are 70 to 80 percent water, that how we program our thoughts affects us physically. If we have limiting beliefs around having enough food to eat, we will continue to draw situations to ourselves that create lack of food. If we do not receive proper nutrition, it will manifest somehow in our physical body. If, on the other hand, we believe there is always enough nutritious food to eat, our bodies will receive the nutrition we need even if we eat smaller meals.

When we change our beliefs, we change our experiences and our DNA. Bruce Lipton, a molecular biologist who has performed extensive research on beliefs and how they change our biology, has shown that our DNA physically changes when we change our core beliefs (Lipton 2005). If the blood of the new covenant was shed to forgive sins, which are nothing more than "wrong thought," then the DNA of the blood of this new covenant must be different from the old. In other words, we are not bound to repeat the sins of our ancestors. This new covenant, which Jesus also referred to as the new kingdom, is enlightenment.

Enlightenment is nothing more than turning on your internal light so that you can see who you truly are. If light carries information and if water is intelligent, then can light be carried by the water in blood? Is this how "bloodline" relates to enlightenment?

The Maya use a term called "blood lightning" to describe the connection between our physical being and spiritual being. When we become congruent, one in spirit and body, we feel this in our heart. Blood lightning, the vital life force that animates consciousness, is also used to describe intuitive knowing or insights that flow through us when we are hardwired to heaven through our heart. It's interesting that the Maya describe this connection with Source as blood lightning. Could they intuitively know that once we follow our heart, the blood is able to carry high frequency light?

J. J. Hurtak writes in *The Book of Knowledge: The Keys of Enoch* (Key 114: 60) that human blood contains consciousness (Hurtak 1987, 136). In their chapter on ascension in *The Masters and the Spiritual Path,* the Prophets say that when we ascend, our blood becomes golden (Prophet 2001, 112). I would say blood (and the water within it) has quite an important role in enlightenment.

Water is so important to brain function and information that people who are born with minimal grey matter in their brains are still able to function normally. According to Nassim Haramein, when water is removed from the brain, consciousness is removed as well (SupremeMasterTV14 2011). Perhaps this is the reason that the human brain is approximately 90 percent water.

Researchers Jibu, Hagan, Hameroff, Pribram, and Yasue studied the properties of microtubules and how they contribute to brain function. They based their work on the premise that microtubules can become coherent because of the structured water within them. They concluded that the quantum nature of the brain's altered states of consciousness is produced by the highly structured water and the quantum electromagnetic field inside the microtubules (Jibu et. al. 1994).

The specific dipole moments and structure of the water within brain cells affects how we think. In addition, this highly aligned water may be a superconductive medium. Superconductivity implies an electrical resistance of exactly zero (zero point again!). This means that electrical energy can flow indefinitely without the addition of energy. Symbolically at a macroscopic level this means when we release all resistance to what is and be in the flow of life through our hearts, we become energy generators! In addition we easily enter altered states of consciousness, which includes all psychic phenomena such as remote viewing, bilocation, and clairaudience.

It is important to note that microtubules have a hexagonal shape, matching the shape of a water crystal. This later led to the belief that consciousness is everywhere in the body. I believe wherever there is structured water, there is consciousness.

When blood and water are in harmonic resonance, they become coherent. The flow of red blood cells through the blood vessels now follows the flow of creation, the caduceus sine wave pattern shown in Chapter 3. This caduceus pattern is an expression of the Golden Mean Ratio, the expression of love. Love is the cause for everything, including the electromagnetic fields produced by the body. As an energy generator and electromagnetic being, you literally magnetize matter to yourself. Blood and water coherence is the key to super-radiance. Don't you love it when science creates a new term and that term superbly describes what in essence is happening within our souls? As you will read in Chapter 8, Eye Am, your body actually becomes super-radiant and glows like the sun. You become golden. I'll talk more about gold later.

Is water crucial to how humans become physically enlightened? What role do blood and the heart play in this?

Since the heart's electromagnetic field is the strongest in the body, it acts like an antenna picking up electromagnetic signals in the form of light, just as your computer receives electromagnetic signals from your internet router. This light enters the heart's field, moves through the heart chakra, and into a very special place in the heart that you will read about in the next chapter. Water within the blood flowing through the heart imprints or downloads the frequency of the incoming electromagnetic radiation (light) and carries the memory of that signal and transfers it to the rest of the body, including DNA. Blood, being an excellent facilitator of electromagnetic waves, easily carries the electromagnetic information imprinted on its water molecules. The water molecules within the microtubules of the cells become coherent with the newly informed water molecules within the blood and download the information to the cells through superradiance, similar to a high speed download.

Emotion has the greatest influence on water, even more than words or sounds. As such, your emotional state can regulate the flow of this information through the body. Negative emotions, such as fear and hate, slow or may even block the flow since negative emotions inhibit heart coherence and thus, superradiance of water. Positive emotions such as love, joy, and gratitude promote coherence in the heart's field and in water. Information is easily transmitted through structured super-radiant water. Hence, the best thing you can do to promote the health of your physical, mental, emotional, and spiritual body is to love yourself.

In *Awakening to Zero Point: The Collective Initiation,* Gregg Braden writes "…Compassion is a quality of feeling, thought and emotion allowing the 1.17 volt liquid crystal circuitry within each of our cells to align with the seven-layered liquid crystal oscillator within our chest that we call 'heart'" (Braden 1997, 156). This alignment of the liquid crystal circuitry from the structured water within the blood flowing through the heart produces one of the most highly regarded attributes of any god or goddess, that of compassion.

Indeed, it is the mingling of sacred blood and water that baptizes us in holy union with the divine. We are hardwired to be God incarnate.

Leviticus 17:11, King James Version (KJV) says *"For the life of a creature is in the blood, and I have given it to you to make atonement for yourselves on the altar, it is the blood that makes atonement for our life."* The word atonement comes from Middle English, *at onement*, meaning in harmony. When we harmonize the energy within our blood and become coherent with the energy of the unified field, we experience all as one because we have direct access to the field through our hearts. It is crucial that we experience this atonement. Once we know and experience beyond the shadow of a doubt that we are all connected, we realize whatever we do to the least of our brothers we do to ourselves.

We are the divine in form.

CHAPTER SIX

The Sacred Coordinate – God's USB Port

*Your soul's treasure chest is buried within the sacred coordinate
in your heart. There you will find the riches of the Universe.*

— *CYCLOPEA*

X marks the spot.

— *UNKNOWN*

As I mentioned in the Introduction, our consciousness is quickly up-grading. Not coincidentally, a cosmic cross occurred in the heavens in August 2010 that was said to have brought with it a time of great spiritual awakening. A cosmic cross is an astrological term, also known as a T-Square, which occurs when at least two planets are opposite each other (180 degrees) and a third forms a square (90 degrees) to the other two planets. In 2010, there were two planets (Saturn and Mars) opposed to *two* other planets (Uranus and Jupiter) that were square a fifth (Pluto). I think what it physically awakened was the human heart, for it is first through the heart that we attain higher consciousness. As Glenda Green writes in, *Love Without End - Jesus Speaks*, our power comes from the heart (Green 2002, 139). Let's look now at how not only the cosmic cross but crosses of all kinds relate to the human heart – from the macrocosm to the microcosm.

The cross is included in many religious and spiritual traditions. A cross is part of the Mayan's Galactic Butterfly. The medicine wheel, a cross within a circle, is used by Native Americans. Peruvians used an equal-armed cross with a superimposed square called the Chakana. In 325 AD the council at Nicea decided to use the traditional symbol of the sun, the cross of light or the sun cross, as the symbol for Christianity. Interestingly, the decision had nothing to do with the Crucifixion.

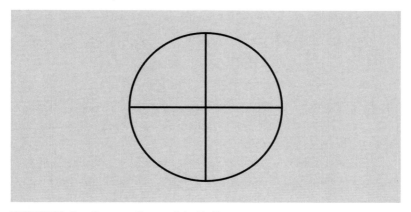

FIGURE 20: Sun Cross or Cross of the Zodiac

The four quadrants within the Sun Cross represent the four seasons. This image is also used in paintings of Jesus and Mary, where it is placed above their heads. I will talk more about this in Chapter 8.

The Coordinate

Whenever two lines intersect, they create a point of intersection and define the position of that point. Think of this point or coordinate as your home base in the Universe. It is your holographic representation of the great central point of the Universe, the singularity of all, or absolute zero point. Of all the infinite combinations of energy in the Universe, this singular combination created your being, your energetic divine blueprint. The combination of energy is a sacred coordination of light and matter that created your essence. Therefore, I call this point the sacred coordinate.

Let's look at the word "coordinate" by breaking it into *co* and *ordinate*. The prefix *co* means coming together mutually, to the same degree. *Ordinate* means to align, consecrate, or ordain. Coordinate, then, means to bring into common action or harmonize. Is it starting to sound familiar, given that you could say that it's about aligning your will with that of the Universe or connecting your heart with the Universe's internet server? The light and matter, the masculine and feminine, the electro and magnetic, the negative and positive charges that coordinated to become your essence: all these naturally conferred holy orders upon you. They ordained you. They consecrated you with your divinity. True ordination is the perfect balance of masculine energy and feminine energy. It all comes back to balance or neutrality – the zero point.

God's USB Connection to the Unified Field or Divine Matrix

The divine matrix or unified zero-point energy field is the framework upon which all matter is formed. It is the divine blueprint of the Universe, and we are part of that Universe.

Mystics have known for centuries that the matrix is the energetic substrate of creation. Everything exists within this main grid. Ancient civilizations knew about the matrix and consciously used it for manifesting. An ancient Mayan document, the Aintiram, shows that the Maya knew of a grid as consisting of 64 squares. Interestingly, this 64 square grid is what Haramein came up with as the shape of the matrix – a cube octahedron (Haramein 2005, 166). The number 64 is also important to us: There are 64 codons in human DNA.

The symbol of the matrix, the Flower of Life (see figure 12), appeared in many ancient cultures, including Egypt, Japan, China, Bulgaria, Turkey, Israel, Spain, Italy, Austria, Morocco, Peru, and Mexico. Ancient forms of prayer and ritual were used to manipulate this energy to produce in physical form the intentions of the participants. The Fruit of Life, depicted below, is taken from the Flower of Life. Its thirteen circles form the basic

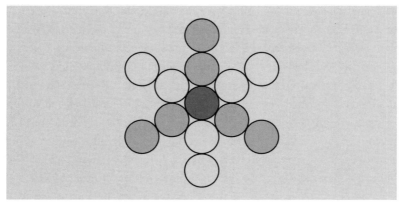

FIGURE 21: Fruit of Life. *(If you look at this three-dimensionally, you will see the x, y, and z axis. Also, it forms an X with a vertical line down the center.)*

blueprint for all atoms, all molecules, and all of matter. It is often referred to as Metatron's Cube, and it is the template from which all of the platonic solids originate.

At the core of your being rests your heart. Again, your heart was the first organ to form when you were a fetus. It is the center point of your being and the origin of the x-y axes of your soul, the place where all creation starts. It is God's USB port to your soul.

Just as the Universe is made up of a grid system, the interior tissue of your heart forms a grid unit. If you look at a cross-section of the heart, you will see that the tissue separating the four chambers forms a cross.

That point of intersection in your heart represents your zero point. You are hardwired to the unified field from this point, your download connection to the divine. This is your soul's address in the Universe, your personal Universal uniform reference locator (URL), your unique set of coordinates and your coordination – your sacred coordinate.

Since this point connects you with the rest of the Universe, it exists inter-dimensionally as well. The patterns your heart creates emanate precisely from this point, just as all of creation emanates from the center circle of the Fruit of Life or the center of the "great" black-white whole. Notice how similar the holographic grid unit of the matrix on page 62 looks to the Fruit of Life.

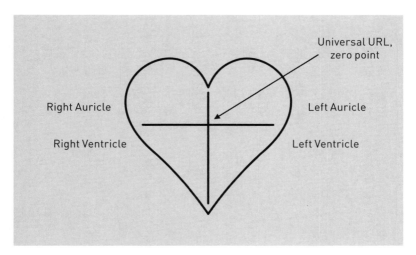

FIGURE 22: The Cross within the Heart

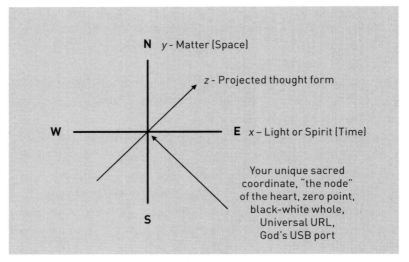

FIGURE 23: Holographic Grid Unit of the Divine Matrix

A holographic representation of your sacred coordinate is also found within other areas of your body, such as your blood. The star attraction for the torus-shaped red blood cell is hemoglobin. It is the iron in the hemoglobin molecule that gives blood its red color. The hemoglobin molecule is made

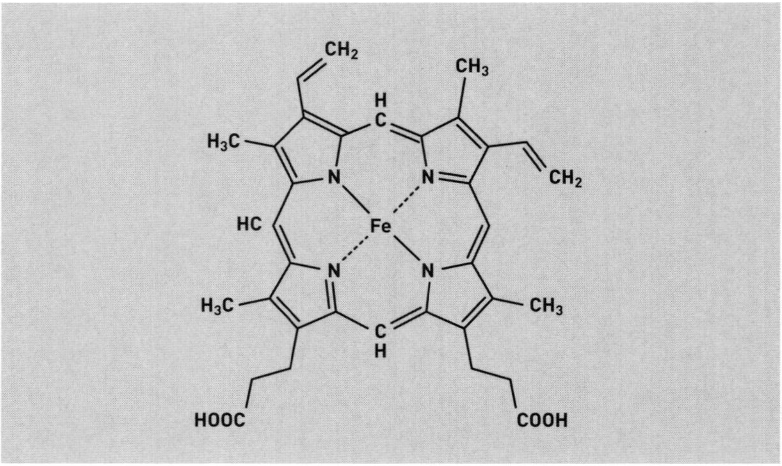

FIGURE 24: Heme Group

up of four subunits, which are in turn made of a protein chain with a non-protein heme group. When you look at how the heme group is arranged, you will see a cross around the iron molecule, Fe, in the center of figure 24. The sacred coordinate is mirrored within every red blood cell!

The sacred coordinate of your heart is like a node. The word node comes from the Latin word nodus, meaning knot or a center point of connection of component parts. It is interesting that the term node is used to describe a bundle of nerves within your heart from which electrical impulses originate, such as the atrioventricular node and sinoatrial node. If you say nodus out loud, it almost sounds like "know this." Indeed, the heart is the seat of wisdom, for it is through this node that you are hardwired to universal intelligence. The term node is also used to describe a point in a standing wave where there is little or no vibration.

This nodal point of the heart mirrors the zero-point energy field, as well as the black-white whole at the center of our galaxy and that of the Universe. Since we live in a holographic Universe, what we find within us we also see in the Universe. The following quote from *A Course in Miracles* denotes the fractal representation of the sacred coordinate to God's heart: "In your heart the heart of God is laid" (Schucman 1996, 368). The heart of God can also be likened to the Great Central Sun.

At the heart of this interdimensional node is a black-white whole that is a holograph representation of Source's original, prime energy or absolute zero-point of the "great" black-white whole. It is your divine spark. As I remind you in *In the Key of Life*, "Take the time to open your heart to yourself, look inside and see the divine spark that has been waiting to be fed" (Cerio 2007, 23).

Everything in the Universe is made up of opposites. A form of this is evidenced in Retired Army LTC Tom Bearden's theory about "isolated charges." He believes a truly isolated charge cannot exist because virtual charges of opposite sign from the vacuum will be attracted to the observable "isolated charge." In the quantum world, when positive and negative charges appear and disappear, they are called virtual charges. As these virtual charges appear and disappear, more virtual charges of opposite sign will surround the observable charge (what we see or experience as a positive or negative charge) producing a polarization or separation of charges of the local vacuum. He calls this a composite dipole (Bearden, 12).

These dipoles are part of what Tom Bearden refers to as "negentropy" or negative entropy (Bearden 2000, 4). If entropy refers to the amount of disorder in a system, then *neg*entropy relates to the ordering of a system. Thus a system built upon composite dipoles is able to reorder charged particles. According to H. E. Puthoff, the source of the vacuum's zero-point energy comes from the motion of charged particles (Puthoff 1989, 4861). Dipoles act as particle oscillators, maintaining a constant flow of charged particles.

The physical heart acts like a dipole oscillator, continuously polarizing and depolarizing. This polarization-depolarization dance feeds the heart's electromagnetic field energy. The sacred coordinate, a microcosm of zero-point energy, contains its own scalar potential for reordering charged particles or Source energy. This comes in handy when you use your heart field to create, which I'll talk more about in Chapter 9, How Creative Energy Works.

Could the sacred coordinate be the Golden Seed Atom within the heart that yogis and other spiritual masters talk about? Could it be a storehouse of your soul's experiences? David Sereda, known for his research using the sound of the sun, postulates that hydrogen holds information (Sereda 2008). If that's true, the implications are astounding, given that hydrogen is the most fundamental and abundant element in the Universe and makes up approximately three-quarters of the sun! Could the hydrogen atoms in your heart act like microchips upon which your akashic records are stored?

Ancient cultures knew about this special place in the heart. They described it as the sacred place within the heart. This term was used in early India in the Upanishads, a series of short writings taken from hymns or teachings. Sufism talks about the secret chamber of the heart where one can join with God. Hinduism also talks about a special place in the heart where God and human may come together in sacred unity. St. Germain through Elizabeth Clare Prophet says this place is not part of the physical heart but is connected to multiple dimensions. He refers to it as a sun or fire within (Prophet 2010, 56-57).

This sacred place or, as I refer to it, this sacred coordinate, is our firewire connection to the divine. It is our connection to Source through our own divine portion of the Universe – the holographic black-white whole within each of our hearts.

Gamma Rays and the Sacred Coordinate

Gamma rays are high-frequency/short-wavelength electromagnetic radiation that contain the most energy of any wave on the electromagnetic spectrum; hence they are the brightest. They originate from stars imploding and forming black holes or when two neutron stars collide. These stars emit intermittent gamma ray bursts that can last from a few milliseconds to several minutes.

Gamma rays are also emitted from the center of our galaxy. As reported by the International Centre for Radio Astronomy Research in early 2013, a group of astronomers from the US, Australia, Italy, and the Netherlands discovered a huge outflow of highly charged particles are coming from the center of our galaxy traveling at supersonic speed. They estimate the amount of energy coming out of the center of our galaxy to be about a million times that of a star going supernova (Staveley-Smith and Gaensler 2013).

In addition to the galactic center, our sun also emits gamma rays during solar flares and coronal mass ejections (CMEs). If the location of the solar flare is on the side of the sun pointing toward Earth, any gamma rays that are emitted travel through space toward the earth. As I pointed out in Chapter 1, we are in the midst of one of the most active solar cycles.

The residual energy/information from these intermittent gamma ray bursts informs the black-white whole within our heart, our mission control center. This intelligent light is instructing the DNA within each of our cells to activate dormant codons (triplet amino acid sequences that code for various proteins). How does this information get to all the cells? As I mentioned in the previous chapter, water within the blood, which passes through the area of the sacred coordinate of the heart, downloads the light codes and "emails" them to all the cells. This is part of the en-lighten-ment process.

Your heart is a mini black-white whole that is connected to every other black-white whole in the Universe. This means all of our hearts are connected and each heart is connected to the galactic center and the "great" black-white whole of the Universe forming God's Universe-wide web.

Like the sun, the heart emits electromagnetic radiation both throughout and from the body. It is the heart's black-white whole that radiates this light. Through its coherent radiance, it orchestrates organized coherent resonance between the cells of the body. It is from this divine spark that your consciousness was birthed and is maintained. The theme song from the movie Titanic was right. The heart does go on and on.

Metatron's Cube

Metatron's Cube (figure 25) is the three-dimensional representation of the holographic grid unit. Notice that the Fruit of Life is the foundation for this cube. If you look at one of the faces of the cube, you will see a vertex at its center. This vertex is formed from the diagonals drawn from each corner of the face. Since a cube has six faces, there are six points of intersection of the diagonals of each face. These points of intersection along with the vertices of the faces of the square correspond to the grid points on the matrix. John 14:2 (KJV), "In my Father's house are many mansions," is easily explained by Metatron's cube. Now imagine millions of Metatron's cubes connected to each other. This forms a three-dimensional grid, with each vertex or point of that grid representing a soul. You have your own unique set of coordinates on the master matrix. This should sound familiar by now!

Perfect harmony and balance are built into Metatron's cube and, therefore, into the matrix. If you extend the vertices of the cube inward they meet at a point that is in perfect balance and harmony within the cube

FIGURE 25: Metatron's Cube

and within the star tetrahedron that is produced by rotating the cube 90 degrees. The lines in our diagram of Metatron's cube connect each vertex to form a star tetrahedron. This inner equidistant point of perfect balance represents the void or nothingness from which everything comes, the ultimate balance point at absolute zero point.

Imagine the torus-shaped Universe comprising a grid system whose fundamental unit of structure is Metatron's cube, the holographic grid unit of the matrix of the Universe. Within each cube is a point of perfect balance which mirrors the absolute zero point at the center of the torus or vacuum. It is from this point, the "God" point, that everything in the Universe is observed and created. This point would not exist without Metatron's cube delineating its coordinate in spacetime.

The holographic grid unit of the matrix consists of the x-axis representing Light and Time and the y-axis representing Matter and Space. This suggests that matter or space is a function of light or time. Indeed light, as a primal form of energy, created matter as pointed out in Chapter 3, A Creative Energy Story.

In that chapter, we saw how light and matter weave together to form a conscious being. This conscious being is created at a unique point on the matrix as defined by the coming together of his/her unique light and matter or his/her unique time and space. This is the heavenly "home" to which many religious and spiritual people refer. It is from this point that the being projects his chosen life experiences for the next life onto the holographic screen of the Universe. It is also from this point that all perspective originates. Since we each have our own coordinate or unique uniform resource locator (URL) on the matrix/web, we see projected reality from our unique perspective, from our *point of view.*

This projection is represented by z on the holographic grid unit. From this projection, your unique grid formed. Everything has its own grid which is essential in maintaining sufficient amounts of life force energy. From this connection point to the unified field, you project your desires and your vision for this lifetime, in concert with the whole of creation, the divine matrix. Since the grid unit is holographic, it also represents your current thoughts projected onto the matrix. As you project your thoughts into the unified field, your thoughts affect time and space, light and matter. As you think, so you become. As I wrote in *In the Key of Life,* "Thought is the vehicle through which manifestation occurs. Creation is a sea of endless potentialities, swimming around until thought comes and catches one" (Cerio 2007, 59).

Creating from the Sacred Coordinate

If Z is a vector projected from your sacred coordinate, then it must have magnitude and direction since, by definition, all vectors has magnitude and direction. Say you are having a dinner party and decide on trout as your main course. Your next projected thought is likely, "Where do I get trout?" This is the direction part of the thought vector. Once you locate the trout, your next projection is how many, the magnitude portion of the vector. Position (direction) and amount (magnitude) are necessary components when manifesting using the grid.

As we project our thoughts into the matrix, we create our version of reality. Yet if we each create our own version of reality from our unique coordinate, on whatever level consciousness grid we are on, how is it that we can coherently communicate with others? How do we all recognize a tall plant with a large trunk and branches with leaves as a tree?

We can because each of us is projecting onto the one unified field. Think of the unified field as a mainframe computer with a huge computer screen. We each project our version of reality onto the screen and what appears is consensus or harmonic reality. The computer or unified field takes into account every detail of every projection everywhere and produces a unified version of the various realities. The field also incorporates its information through the feedback loop or self-reflexive nature of the torus-shaped Universe. From this consensus model of the Universe, it is easy to see that we are all co-creators of our larger reality.

Scalar Waves

Unlike vectors, scalar waves have magnitude with no direction. Scalar waves are standing electromagnetic waves. We talked about standing waves when we talked about nodes. Here is a little lesson about standing waves.

Every object has a natural frequency of resonance when struck or otherwise disturbed. These natural frequencies are associated with standing waves. Only certain wave frequencies will produce standing waves. When an object resonates or vibrates, the resonance forms standing waves within the object. What all this scientific jargon is saying is that an object's natural resonance is nothing more than the harmonic frequencies of the standing wave patterns within the object. An object will choose a small range of frequencies at which to vibrate that result in the highest wave amplitude with the lowest input of energy, thus receiving maximum benefit from minimum effort. Think back to Chapter 2, A 'Hole' New World. What do standing waves sound like? (Pardon the pun.) Yes! Zero-point energy! And what kind of standing waves are we concerned with? Scalar waves.

Scalar waves are said to exist in a vacuum and do not exist in the material world. They "fill the void" of black-white wholes, nodes, and – hearts, all of which are both empty and full at the same time. Unlike scalar waves, longitudinal waves and transverse waves (such as sine waves) do exist in the physical world. Examples of transverse waves are waves on a string or waves in a lake. Sound traveling through air or the wave through a slinky® are examples of longitudinal waves.

According to Nicola Tesla, longitudinal scalar waves exist between the ends of a dipole and it is partly through this phenomenon that he discovered free energy. Scalar waves are the expression of nonlocal reality. They are the vehicle through which Prime Creator changes the form of energy.

Understanding scalar waves is fundamental to understanding what I call my Translation Equation of Matter. "In the beginning was the Word and the Word was with God and the Word was God" (John 1:1, KJV). The Word is sound. Pythagoras referred to the sound coming from the Universe as the Music of the Spheres. Remember the Big Bang Theory? There must have been a huge amount of sound! Anyway, the first and primal form of energy is sound and that's where my Translation Equation begins.

If all form comes from the energy of the cosmic womb of creation, the "great" black-white whole, how does it change from sound to light to physical matter? The answer is through scalar waves. Whenever we manifest, we are using scalar wave technology. And once something is in the physical, how does it go back into essential energy? How do we go from a physical body to our light body? It happens through translation.

I chose that word because of its various meanings. One definition of translation is to change into another form, or transform. Another is to convey or remove from Earth to heaven without dying and a third, archaic meaning is to transport or enrapture.

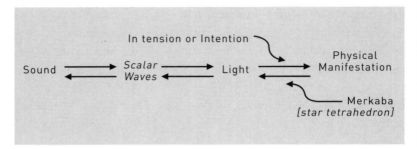

FIGURE 26: Translation Equation

After studying my translation equation in figure 26, you may be wondering what a merkaba is. It's your light-spirit body. This body has a particular form, as does everything in the Universe. (I think by now you are getting this point!) The shape of the merkaba around your body is that of the star tetrahedron. If you remember in Chapter 3, A Creative Energy Story, we talked about the star tetrahedron inscribed in a circle as the primal sacred geometry template used by the Universe.

A tetrahedron is a three-dimensional equilateral triangle with four sides. Since it is equilateral, all sides are the same length and all interior angles are 60 degrees. A star tetrahedron is a three-dimensional Star of David consist-

FIGURE 25: Three-Dimensional Star Tetrahedron Drawn from the *Fruit of Life*

ing of two tetrahedrons placed within one another as shown in figure 27. Notice that this shape is the same shape that is contained within the circle in figure 13 on page 37. The star tetrahedron is the foundational form through which space divides itself.

This shape also derives from Metatron's Cube, as depicted in figure 25. Interestingly, *3 Enoch*, an Old Testament Apocryphal book, also known as *The Revelation of Metatron* (when Enoch ascended into heaven, he became archangel Metatron), is part of the Merkabah texts.

So why is the merkaba part of my Translation Equation? Merkaba, also spelled merkabah, means chariot or throne in Hebrew. Ezekiel 1:4-26, which describes the glory of God with bright light and fire, speaks about a chariot that has wheels within wheels with a *human* likeness seated on its throne. I believe the merkaba is your vehicle of ascension and a means of returning to your light body. In other words, it takes the energy back to its essential, nonphysical state – back to its divine origin.

According to the Translation Equation, energy starts as vibration or sound and, through scalar waves, changes its form into light. In physics, tension, or a pulling force, can also be viewed as a *separating* force. So tension or, in this case, *in*tention, creates the force needed both to slow the vibration of particles enough in order to produce the physical and to separate it from its source or unified field in order to manifest a discrete, unique physical object with its own coordinates on the grid. Since the unified field is consciousness, it naturally forms intention. Since you are part of the unified field, your intentions have the power to manifest in the physical.

What else do we need to manifest in the physical?

CHAPTER SEVEN

Turning On Your Heart's Light

*The light from a million candles cannot compare
to the light that shines from an awakened heart.*

— *CYCLOPEA*

Within the sacred coordinate of the heart lies a holographic sun like the sun in our solar system and the Great Central Sun of the Universe. Contained within the sacred coordinate is the original divine spark from which our unique energy emerged. As I wrote in *In the Key of Life*, we are each apportioned a unique piece of eternal Source energy: *"You are the individuated genius from an energy matrix from the vast Source of All [zero-point energy, the singularity]. No one has the exact same manifestation of codes as you. You have your own unique resonant blueprint in the cosmos"* (Cerio 2007, 63).

Our individual divine matrix was formed from the One Source of All, the absolute zero point or prime singularity of the "great" black-white whole. It is the primal etheric template from which all of our other templates form. This individual divine matrix is the blueprint from which every facet of our lives emerges.

Its orientation in the unified field is governed by the sacred coordinate. The ordinates of this point on the master grid contain your unique codes that unlock the doors of manifestation for you and you alone. How, then, do we open the door to this treasure chest? Before we can access the goodie drawer, we have some work to do. Would you give your teenager the keys to your car without first teaching him how to drive? With power comes responsibility and a level of maturity. The same is true for manifesting. If the storehouse to creation were to be opened to us before we were responsible and mature enough, we could destroy ourselves, our family, or the planet. It is like putting a loaded gun in the hands of a three-year-old.

The work we must do is our inner work of cleaning out our worn out beliefs closet, vacuuming up stuck emotions, removing the cobwebs from our minds, and polishing the mirrors to our souls so we see who we truly are. This 24/7 house cleaning job comes with no holidays, vacation days, or sick days. It can be tedious, tough, and tiring…and it is the most important work that we will ever do.

Just as a sculptor chips away the marble that covers the already-formed work of art, our inner work is to remove what doesn't belong and what is not in resonance with our authentic selves. Put another way, within each of our hearts is a gift. It is up to us to unwrap it.

How we go about this process is unique for each individual and is not the subject of this book, though I cover aspects of it in *In the Key of Life*. Yoga, Tai Chi, and Qi Gong are also among the excellent tools available to you to clear your body of stagnant chi, quiet your mind, free up the flow of Source energy, and strengthen your intuition. Here, though, I will assume that you are already in process with that inner work. Instead, I will focus on how we can activate our inner light, which comes from both your heart and the high heart.

Luckily for us, the Universe is providing assistance. According to the Lawrence Berkley Laboratory's Muller and Rohde, there is an increase in genus biodiversity every 62 million years (Rohde and Muller 2005, 210), and I think we are currently at the crest of a new 62 million year cycle, since we are ripe for a major overhaul. While Muller and Rohde aren't sure what causes this, David Wilcock, an intuitive and consciousness science researcher, thinks that it is light wave propagations from the center of our galaxy that are driving this evolutionary change (Wilcock 2011). After all, information and light are synonymous. As I pointed out in the Introduction, these light waves rewrite our DNA to program it to change our characteristics, consciousness, and behavior.

Cosmic Defibrillator

Now that we know how light is transported through the body, what happens in the heart that turns on its "heart light?" Where does the light that the heart emits come from?

The black-white whole at the galactic center pulses waves of light like a heartbeat. These waves may contain gamma ray bursts coming from the galactic center. Such bursts would act like a cosmic defibrillator, jump-starting our heart's sun to emit higher frequency light. It stands to reason that our heart's electromagnetic field would change as well, perhaps becoming larger and stronger. As you will learn in the next chapter, short gamma ray bursts produce copious amounts of gold. Now that could make your heart shine!

Eternal Internal Flame

You are a conscious being of light. Light is your source and essence. Realizing that you are light is like having been born blind, having then regained your vision and being now able to see your physical self for the first time. Of course, you have been you all along, even though you couldn't see what you look like. Now that you can, a major aspect of who you are has suddenly been revealed to you. This aspect is no surprise to others, who could see you all along. But until you removed your blinders, you were, well, blind. This is the job each of us came to do – to remove the filters that have clouded our perception of ourselves.

Our internal pilot light has always been burning. It is the same flame depicted in art and statues within the sacred hearts of Jesus and Mary. At the core of who we are is a mini sun that has been there since our birth. It is our internal and eternal light, our divine spark. This spark starts as a glowing ember. But it is up to us to fuel this spark with passion and provide the energy needed to power God's USB port.

Passion is fire energy. What does your heart love to do above all other things? This is your passion. When we follow the calling of our hearts and live our passion, we stoke the fire within our hearts. Eventually, this divine spark ignites. It is the energy from this internal inferno that fuels our enthusiasm. The more enthusiasm is created, the more energy is available for us to manifest our passion in the physical.

We have all experienced the energy that comes from being excited about something. This is the energy that keeps you up until late at night and gets you back out of bed at dawn, raring to go. You seem to have an endless supply of energy and feel able to leap tall buildings in a single bound!

Being in love creates passion whether it is love for another or love for your work or for some project. It is the vibration of love that starts the wheels of passion turning and gets the fire energy burning. Without first feeling this in our hearts, our sparks cannot ignite. Love is the ignition source for all of creation.

We begin by loving ourselves. This includes loving our human selves and those characteristics that make us human, from our vast array of emotions to our indomitable spirit. It also includes loving our divine selves, our true nature as the embodied gods and goddesses that the masters tell us we are. When we make the inner like the outer and the outer like the inner, when our human and divine selves become congruent, we enter the kingdom, which is nothing other than the sacred coordinate within the heart. When we connect our internal USB port to heaven, all things are possible because we are logged into the cosmic computer. We have cracked the code, and the keys to the kingdom are ours.

Only once we love all of who we are, are we able to do the same with others. In so doing, we acknowledge on a deep level that we are all part of the unified field of creation. Each of us is a mirror, reflecting an aspect of another. We are each a piece of the holographic puzzle of unity consciousness. Once we download our divinity, we lose the ego identity of separation. As our love becomes super-radiant, we acknowledge our divine place in the cosmos.

We live as the gods and goddesses that we are when we "come from our hearts." We literally orient ourselves through our unique sacred coordinates to the divine matrix so that we are in direct communication with unity consciousness – hardwired to heaven. We become "wise beyond our years" because when we enter the black-white whole of our heart, we break free of space-time and enter the infinite timeless beauty of divine creation.

It is through knowing that we are God *and* experiencing it that we activate the divine spark within the sacred coordinate of our hearts. Our passion for living our divinity provides the fuel necessary to ignite the spark into a flame that burns within our hearts.

The Sun/Son of God that we are is the holographic representation of the sun from our solar system and the Great Central Sun. We glow from our hearts. We become radiant like the sun. As it says in the Gospel of Thomas (Saying 24), "His disciples said, 'Show us the place where you are, for we must seek it.' He said to them, 'Anyone here with two ears better listen! There is a light within a person of light, and it shines on the whole world. If it does not shine, it is dark'" (Miller 1994, 310). Once this light is illuminated, we are enlightened. This is Christ Consciousness.

Igniting and Aligning the High Heart

Once this spark is ignited, the energy travels up to the high heart, located near the thymus gland. The thymus, a couple of inches (5cm) below the notch of the sternum and behind the sternum, produces T-lymphocytes (disease-fighting white blood cells) that are essential for a healthy immune system. Think of your heart as the doorway that, when fully open, allows light from the sacred coordinate to shine on your high heart. Once this line of energy is activated, it opens a clear channel of communication or a local area network (LAN), between our physical heart, high heart, and brain.

This connection is crucial for the balanced functioning of the heart and mind. When we become slaves to our mind and forget to think with our hearts, we see the results in the current state of the world. Once we think with our hearts and use our minds to interpret what our hearts have chosen to create, we create from the harmonic resonance of love.

At the high heart we are "immune" to lower consciousness thought forms. We are untouchable by any outside influences. We are sovereign unto ourselves, each a god incarnate.

The high heart is a repository for the tiniest units of matter. In *Love without End - Jesus Speaks*, Glenda Green refers to the fundamental elements of matter as "adamantine particles" (Green 2002, 38). Adamantine particles, she says, have an innate intelligence to manifest any substance, but they require energy to arrange them – the energy of love (Green 2002, 89). Not human love but divine love, a love that comes with the conscious awareness of the truth of who we are.

Our shift in consciousness from human beings to divine beings is what opens the door to the cosmic toy chest! Now that the Tinker Toys of creation lay before us, we can enter the unified field through scalar waves and access the codes of creation. We can experience ourselves as the creator gods and goddesses we always have been.

CHAPTER EIGHT

Eye Am

And God said unto Moses, I am that I am...
— *EXODUS 3:14, KING JAMES VERSION*

If God is the great "I AM," then who are we? What if we are God incarnate, like Jesus was? Before you reject this idea as blasphemy, consider the many ancient cultures that believed star beings (extraterrestrials) to be gods because they descended from the sky with supernatural-seeming advanced technology. Is it all just a matter of perspective? Whose perspective and from what vantage point? In the end, the only true vantage point is our own, since each of us has a unique perspective of reality. We have our own set of truths, which change as our perspective changes.

That perspective comes from how we perceive the world through our five senses. Most of us, when touching, viewing, smelling, hearing and tasting a red apple, would report similar, if not identical experiences. It is red and round. It feels smooth and firm. It has a faint sweet smell. It makes a crunching noise when we bite into it and tastes sweet and juicy.

But what about our so-called "sixth sense?" Would using it bring about different experiences of that apple? What if one person could see in his mind's eye that the apple came from a farmer's tree? What if another knew that this apple had been picked by a young girl? Yet another person might hear the song the young girl was singing when she picked it. The picture of this apple could well be different for each of us when we use our own sixth sense, an inner sense that comes from our seat of intuition, which to most mystics and religions is the third eye chakra or pineal gland.

The "Eye" of the I AM

The pineal gland, known as "the seat of the soul," a term coined by Descartes, is a raisin-sized, reddish-purple endocrine gland located in the center of the brain between the two hemispheres. It is not isolated by the blood-brain barrier and, in fact, the pineal gland is second only to the kidneys in blood flow. Just as the heart is the first fetal organ to form, the pineal is the first gland to form within the embryo. Scientists are still discovering what functions this pine cone-shaped gland carries out. What they do know is that the hormone melatonin is produced in the pineal gland. Melatonin regulates wake/sleep patterns and how we respond to varying amounts of daylight as the seasons change. What is interesting about this hormone is that it is secreted during times of darkness.

Dr. Rick Strassman believes that the hallucinogenic chemical dimethyltryptamine or DMT, which he calls the spirit molecule, is also produced by the pineal gland (Strassman 2001, 55, 69). It is still difficult to say for certain that DMT is produced within the pineal gland since its half-life is fifteen minutes (a half-life is the time it takes for half of the substance to disintegrate). Strassman speculates that DMT is secreted from the pineal gland during near-death experiences (Strassman 2001, 326).

Others say DMT may be secreted when the pineal gland is stimulated or awakened during kundalini awakenings, as well as at other times. There is further speculation that during this time of Shift, the pineal gland is producing increased levels of DMT due to Earth's decreasing magnetic field and the increasing solar activity. If DMT is the spirit molecule, as Strassman calls it, the Universe is offering mass injections of it to wake us up.

Activation of the pineal gland can occur through various ways, such as meditation, lucid dreaming, stimulation of the roof of the mouth with the tongue, and even from a head injury, since vibration of the gland is crucial to its awakening. An excellent source of vibration for opening the pineal gland is sound. Alfred Tomatis, an otolaryngologist, found that vocal harmonics such as Gregorian chants, charge the central nervous system and the cortex of the brain. Over the centuries, indigenous cultures and many religions have used this vibrational technology in their chants and songs. Chanting OM or AUM is thought to provide the proper vibration of the cranial bones to awaken the pineal. Vocal toning acts as a vibrator of the gland, causing it to move at faster speeds. Some believe that the increased vibratory rate of the pineal gland allows us to tap into altered states of consciousness (Silva 2002, 225).

An August 12, 2004 NIH News press release reported that Dr. Klein, of the National Institute for Child Health and Human Development, found that human pineal gland cells closely resemble the photoreceptor cells in the retina of the eye. The press release stated that the photoreceptor cells of the pineal gland in some mammals, such as frogs and birds, can sense light. In addition, the retina of these mammals can produce small amounts of melatonin, the chemical that is known to be produced in the human pineal gland (NIH Press Release 2004 and Klein 2004, 264). Could this explain how we are able to see colors and images in our third eye when our eyes are closed? Perhaps this is how the word insight originated!

Communication Tower

Calcite crystals and, quite possibly DMT crystals, have been found in a watery fluid within the gland, turning the pineal gland into a liquid crystal tuner. What could the pineal gland's liquid crystal be tuning into? According to David Wilcock, it is tuning into the unified field, or as he calls it, the Source Field. He suggests that not only is it tuning into signals from the field, it is also transmitting signals (Wilcock 2011). What is this flow of information all about? Who are we communicating with and why?

Have you ever seen an aura or an apparition? Have you heard someone call you but no one is around? Have you smelled perfume that a deceased loved one wore? Have you seen images, shapes, or words with your eyes closed? Have you felt a presence, as though someone were standing next to you? Could the pineal gland be a direct line of communication with other dimensions?

Water Is the Gate

Darkness is needed to initiate electromagnetic activity in the pineal gland. If you have ever meditated, you probably noticed that it is easier to see colors, shapes, etc., in your third eye if the room is dark. This electromagnetic activity can feel like a pressure inside your head, or you may hear tones or a buzz similar to what you hear near high tension wires.

Clusters of magnetite, the most magnetic of all naturally-occurring minerals on Earth, have been found just outside of the pineal gland. A group of three researchers found that the pineal gland plays a role in our sense of direction. They wonder if the magnetite in human brains plays a role in sensing direction similar to that in other animals, such as birds and dolphins (Bayliss, Bishop, and Fowler 1985, 1759). There is speculation that this magnetite acts to sensitize us to the earth's electromagnetic field. According to David Wilcock, once an electromagnetic field is formed within the pineal, it protects the water within it from all other electromagnetic fields (Wilcock 2011). This is crucial because one of the functions of water is to receive information from light and, by restructuring itself, transfer that information to the body. Remember, it is the form that informs. Water tunes into cosmic consciousness by structuring itself to again allow for superradiance and nonlocality, meaning that information can travel superfast between structured water molecules and inform distant water molecules that are separated in space.

Dr. Stuart Hameroff believes that our consciousness can exist outside the body, based on his knowledge of microtubules within the neurons of the brain. He suggested that consciousness may be able to leave the microtubules of one body at the time of death and eventually enter another body when that consciousness is reincarnated (*Miracle Detectives,* Oprah Winfrey Network, 2011).

Remember that the most important part of the microtubule is that it is filled with water! Because of it, you (your consciousness) are now able to travel to different dimensions or travel astrally. I believe this phenomenon is what makes remote reviewing and bilocation possible. Water is the gateway through which higher consciousness flows. Without the unique properties of water, we could not access our multidimensionality.

In 2010, a group of six scientists, including virologist Luc Montagnier, took a piece of HIV DNA, made multiple copies of it, put it in a test tube, and then diluted it with water until an electromagnetic signal was detected. The contents of the tube were filtered. A second tube filled with pure water was also diluted and filtered in the same manner as the first tube. Both tubes were subjected to extremely low electromagnetic radiation for eighteen hours. It was noted that both tubes were now emitting electromagnetic signals. To the second tube, they then added DNA polymerase (an enzyme needed in the production of DNA), nucleotides (components of DNA), and primers and the reaction was assisted by the addition of heat. To their surprise, the second tube now contained DNA, which was 98 percent identical to the DNA in the first tube. A conclusion from this experiment was that some bacterial and viral DNA can create extremely low frequency electromagnetic signals when highly diluted in water (Montagnier et. al. 2010). Montagnier wondered about water's role in all this since in an earlier experiment he had seen bacteria grow from aqueous solutions that were thought to be sterile. He partially attributed the phenomenon to some of water's unusual properties such as its ability to form long chains of dipoles (Montagnier et. al. 2009, 89).

It seems that the water bound to the DNA molecule containing the in-form-ation of that particular DNA sequence sent a signal via extremely low frequency electromagnetic waves to the water in the second tube that was capable of arranging the building blocks of DNA to form almost an exact copy of the one in the first tube. Could the strand of DNA have been woven together by the vortex-like motion of water that may have been created by the low frequency electromagnetic field, producing the spiraling form of its intended result: the spiral molecule DNA?

Science once looked at water as an innocent bystander not usually partaking in reactive fun. As biologists delve deeper into the mystery of life they are finding that water is a crucial component in many, if not most, physiological reactions.

Perhaps the pineal gland, with its DMT and its calcite and near-by magnetite antenna, receives information from the heart, whose black-white whole is attuned to its fractal counterparts, the sun and the galactic center. Their intermittent gamma ray bursts of highly charged particles imprint this information through the sacred coordinate into the heart. From there it is carried by water in the blood to the pineal gland. The pineal gland, if you will recall, is second in terms of blood flow of all the body's organs. The water within the blood then informs the water within the pineal gland. The water within the blood was informed through the higher vibration of light, which is carried to the pineal.

This is why vibration of the pineal gland is so important to its awakening. This vibration causes the vortex-like movement of water within the gland. The vortex shape of the gland provides the perfect environment for this movement. In turn, this water informs its mirror spiral form within the body, DNA.

In March 2011, researchers Hassan Khesbak, Olesya Savchuk, Satoru Tsushima, and Karim Fahmy, discovered that the surface of DNA is covered with water molecules in a specific way and concluded that water affects the structure of DNA (Khesbak et al. 2011, 5834). Could the water molecules in Montagnier's experiment have downloaded the information from the DNA in the first tube and emailed the water molecules in the second tube to construct an almost exact copy of the DNA in the first tube? Additionally, perhaps the information that water imparts to DNA awakens the dormant codons within the double helix, effectively rewriting and encrypting our DNA with the keys to the kingdom of multidimensional awareness. This may explain how the human body and consciousness is evolving during this momentous time on Earth.

When the caterpillar returns to its elemental self, a watery substance, as part of its metamorphosis, it is this water that wakes up the imaginal cells in that pool to turn on certain genes and begin the formation of the butterfly. Water is the medium through which the language of light is written.

The Pineal-Blood-Gold Connection

Gold is considered the most precious of all precious metals, so precious that it has been used to back paper money. It is precious not only because it is so rare on Earth, but because it is equally rare throughout the Universe. The reason is that gold is only produced during the rarest, hottest, most powerful explosion in the Universe: when two neutron stars collide and go supernova and produce short gamma ray bursts.

A team of astrophysicists, Berger, Fong, and Chornock, recently found the evidence they sought to link short gamma ray bursts to neutron star collisions. Edo Berger, of the Harvard-Smithsonian Center for Astrophysics, reported in a July 17, 2013 press conference that these short gamma ray bursts produce massive amounts of gold. He believes this is where all the gold in the Universe originates. All of the gold on Earth came from collisions that occurred over 4 ½ billion years ago before the dawn of our solar system. The amount of gold produced in the supernovae events is estimated to be ten times the mass of the moon (Harvard-Smithsonian Center for Astrophysics 2013). That's one big gold strike!

Gold is also known for its useful qualities. It is malleable and ductile, meaning it is easily shaped and drawn into wire, and does not oxidize, making it rust- or corrosion-resistant. While not inert, it is the least chemically reactive of all the metals. It is thus a good conductor of electricity and readily forms alloys with other metals.

Its chemical symbol, Au, comes from the Latin word *aurum*, meaning shining down. Its symbol "☉" is also the astrological symbol for the sun. The Incas called gold the "sweat from the sun." The Aztecs believed gold to be a product of the gods or an alchemical excrement. Gold has also been associated with perfect or divine principles such as the Golden Mean. Can your blood become golden? How do you attain a "heart of gold?" Does our blood contain gold when we become God incarnate?

Monoatomic or white powder gold is used to activate the pineal gland (third eye chakra) and the crown chakra and to purify and balance the heart chakra. How can the pineal gland be opened by taking gold powder, given that gold is not at all related to DMT or any other hallucinogenic drugs?

If we don't ingest it, where does the gold come from? When we open our third eye and see as the god that we are sees, we open the floodgates of light. If the eye is a device for focusing light, the third eye focuses the light of heaven that comes through the heart. The beam of light is the vector through which gold makes its debut in the body. Liquid crystalline light beams form within the heart itself.

As I explained in Chapter 5, the light that enters the heart is carried through the blood via water. Remember that gold is formed by short gamma ray bursts? Could these gamma rays carry the ingredients for gold and impart the energy of gold into your blood?

As this enlightened blood travels through the blood vessels, it does so in the caduceus sine wave pattern or vortex-like motion. This spinning of the red blood cells creates the perfect electromagnetic field where no energy is lost; rather, the energy is conserved and increased through the influx of this crystallized light. You might say that you "weave a web of gold" within your blood. Manna/itz/monoatomic gold forms from this spinning vortex within your blood. It is the precipitate from heaven, the crystallized dew from the Great Central Sun. Once this golden energy forms within the blood, it acts as a doorstop, keeping open the keys to the kingdom.

Blood is life-giving and sustaining, and once we become enlightened alchemists, we literally become golden. Look at it this way. If you take out the "I" in gold and place it in front of the remaining letters, you get **I god**. Okay, so I changed the font. But you get my drift. By the way, El or (L), a Hebrew word for God, is in the middle of gold! I AM God. Yes, dears. You *are* God incarnate. I guess gold is really precious!

The Pineal-Heart Connection

When the pineal gland is stimulated through various ways, as noted above, it secretes a liquid that has been referred to as ambrosia, living water, and amrita, a Sanskrit word that means immortality. This divine elixir apparently travels from the pineal gland through the sphenoid cavity to the roof of the mouth at the area where the soft and hard palates meet. Interestingly, the embryologic development of the pineal gland originates from the epithelial thickening of tissue from the roof of the oral cavity that becomes the mouth. One way to stimulate the flow of this liquid is by stimulation of the roof of the mouth with the tongue.

The tip of the tongue is the first tissue to differentiate from the heart in a human embryo. The tongue, therefore, is linked to the heart and to creative energy. When we speak, we are using one form of creative energy and when we speak from our heart, we are speaking our truth directly from Source.

By using the tongue to activate the release of the amrita, we are connecting the energy pathway between the heart and the pineal gland. Once the pineal is open, consciousness expands into no time, through past, present, and future, and from one dimension to another.

The energy for the pineal activation comes up from the sacral chakra or "golden stove," as it is known in Chinese alchemy, through the heart chakra or the heart to the third eye chakra or pineal gland. The golden stove is also known as the lower dantian. Dantian is a Chinese word that loosely translated means elixir field. In Taoist meditative practices, the "White Drop" or energy from the secretion by the pineal gland (the upper dantian) goes to the heart (the middle dantian) and mixes with the "Red Drop" or heat generated from the sacral chakra (the lower dantian), then rises to the middle dantian. When these "two drops" or energies merge in the heart, they produce the experience of emptiness or a still mind. This state of mind is equivalent to tapping into the Tao or the Creator. It is an enlightened mind. You enter the temple of the heart – the inner sanctum or the sacred coordinate. The goal of Chinese alchemists was to become immortal through the ingestion of alchemically produced gold. Can the body do the alchemy for us?

It is thought that oxytocin, the feel-good hormone that is released during orgasm, is part of the amrita. Oxytocin is stored in the pituitary gland. The pituitary joins in the fun with the pineal gland during the awakening of the third eye. Some say that the pineal gland and the pituitary gland must vibrate in unison to produce the electromagnetic field of the opened third eye. A group of six scientists found that when oxytocin comes in contact with specific locations in the atria or upper chambers of rat hearts it releases atrial natriuretic cardiac hormone (Gutkowska et al. 1997, 11704).

Scientists use mice and rats in their research because their genetic and biological makeup is similar to humans. What if oxytocin releases atrial natriuretic hormone in humans? If this is so, why would activating the pineal gland stimulate the heart to produce a hormone that stimulates the production of urine (in the kidneys) and the excretion of sodium? Could it be that the energy from the activated pineal gland (upper dantian) flows to the heart (middle dantian) and then to the sacral chakra where the kidneys are located (lower dantian)? The energy cascades down to the next lower dantian like water falling from pool to pool. "You anoint my *head with oil, my cup overflows*" (Psalm 23:5 KJV). The oil is the amrita and what overflows is the electromagnetic energy of fully activated third eye, heart, and sacral chakras. "*Surely goodness and mercy shall follow me all the days of my life, and I will dwell in the house of the Lord forever*" (Psalm 23:6 KJV). Once you attain this level of vibration, you magnetize your heart's desire, your goodness and mercy. You dwell within the sacred coordinate of your heart and enter the kingdom of God, which is unbounded by time and space.

The Aramaic word, *rahm*, which I'll talk more about in the next chapter, means a radiant or shining love. Neil Douglas-Klotz in his book, *The Hidden Gospel: Decoding the Spiritual Message of the Aramaic Jesus*, breaks down the word rahm into its Aramaic roots: *RA*, meaning shining, and *ChM*, meaning our dark interior (Douglas-Klotz 2001, 143). It is easy to see how this word is connected to the pineal gland activation. Once the pineal is activated, there is light shining in the dark interior. This light is radiant *love*, love that comes through the heart. If you chant rahm over and over, it will stimulate your pineal gland similar to chanting AUM.

The "Eye" of the Catholic Church

For centuries, spiritual leaders from every background have been aware of the power of awakening the pineal gland. Buddhists, Hindus, Muslims, indigenous tribes all around the world, and even Popes may have known about this key. Since Catholicism is the religion with which I am most familiar, let's look at where the Catholic Church "hides" this life-changing information.

In the picture of Our Lady of Victory Basilica in Lackawanna, New York (figure 28), Mother Mary is standing in the background with two angels kneeling on either side of her. Directly in front of her and between the angels is a pine cone. Yes, a pine cone. Did you know there is a huge bronze pine cone in the Vatican Museum's courtyard? When I asked the basilica tour guide why there were pine cones at the Vatican and at the basilica (above the main entrance and as a finial on the bottom of the chandeliers in the vestibule), he didn't know. Neither did a gentleman on the tour who had completed several years of seminary. Both suggested that a pine cone represents seeds and new growth. Whether or not there is any truth in that explanation, there is clearly a deeper meaning behind the Catholic Church's use of the pine cone.

Look again at the picture of the basilica. You'll see that I drew three lines on it: one across each of the angels' backs and one from the midsection of the pine cone up Mary's midsection. These lines intersect at her third eye.

FIGURE 28: Main Entrance to Our Lady of Victory Basilica near Buffalo, NY
(Photo Joan Cerio, lines added by author)

Even the geometry of the artwork points to the importance of the third eye. This geometry looks very much like the chi rho or christogram depicted in figure 29. Note that the three lines are a depiction of the holographic grid unit.

I believe the Church may use the pine cone to symbolize the pineal gland, the gateway to accessing the sacred coordinate within our hearts.

Mother Mary is usually drawn with a golden halo or a mandorla. The mandorla is the aura or bio-field around her body. How does the mandorla or halo form?

With the activation of the pineal gland, our inner sight is awakened. The pineal gland is the "eye of the heart." It acts like a periscope through which we see our connection to the unified field from our sacred coordinate. The "P" portion of the christogram looks like a periscope; the "P" could also stand for periscope or pineal. I love it when words and symbols work together! The energy from awakened kundalini springs up through all the chakras and out the crown, preparing the crown for connection with higher dimensions. This also provides the energetic opening for the pineal gland to receive higher dimensional information through its "periscope."

FIGURE 29: Photo of Ancient Mosaic Christogram behind Mary's Head *(Courtesy of Wikipedia®, Udimu)*

The pineal gland now acts as a radio tower with an antenna, receiving information that, prior to its awakening, would have been at too high a vibration to be discerned. Until the pineal gland is activated, higher information cannot be coherently projected into the brain's electromagnetic field. Fear is nothing more than the brain's inability to harmonize or make coherent what appears to be chaotic information. Once the brain is able to harmonize with the higher vibratory information it once considered chaotic, and once it sends this coherent information to the heart, we become fearless. God incarnate has no fear.

Now that the heart is receiving coherent signals from the brain, the heart's EM field becomes more coherent and brighter. This step up in energy allows you to enter your sacred coordinate and connect God's USB cable. Once this connection is established, Source light beams from your heart creating the mandorla or golden bio-field around your body. This is why Jesus is depicted with his finger pointing to the heart. This golden light pops out of the sacred coordinate and forms its fractal counterpart, the halo that is depicted over the heads of angels, saints, Jesus, and Mary. "*The light of the body is the eye; if therefore thine eye be single, thy whole body shall*

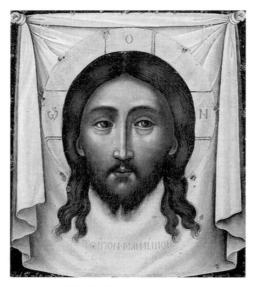

FIGURE 30: Jesus with Halo

be full of light" (Matt 6:22, KJV). The halo shows the sacred coordinate within the sun or golden glow that is physically surrounding the heads of the masters.

The sacred heart is usually painted with flames, the light that comes from the holographic sun within your heart's sacred coordinate. The symbol for the sun cross is the same as for the halo because the sun of God that you are is now shining on the outside as well as the inside. You are now congruent with the high frequency energy of the divine.

If the Popes knew about the importance of the pineal gland, why didn't the Catholic Church tell its parishioners about this and give them the tools to "turn on their heart lights?" Better yet, why did the Catholic Church allow its architecture and paintings to be encoded with the keys to awakening our divinity? Did the Church know that someday this empowering information would be made public, so it kept the codes in plain sight, the best place to hide something? It did not speak about what the pine cones represent.

If the people were misled about how to "enter the kingdom" and if alternative interpretations of the Bible were sanctioned, Church fathers could keep the parishioners as followers of Christ instead of empowered gods and goddesses who would follow only their own inner guidance. Control and power over the people could mean the Church could amass power and wealth. The Bible quotes Jesus as saying "*Verily, verily, I say unto you, He that believes in me, the works that I do shall he do also; and **greater works than these shall he do** [author's emphasis]; because I go unto my Father*" (John 14:12, KJV). We, too, shall go unto our Father, the sacred coordinate within, and connect with our divine birthright.

So who are we? Each of us, through our sacred coordinate, is a wondrous coordination of light and flesh whose spiritual home base is a coordinate on the divine matrix. When we actualize and live our divine essence we are given the keys to the kingdom. We are logged into the Creator's computer. We are all God's children. God, the unified field, is our Creator and Source of All. We are not God, for the whole is greater than the sum of its parts. Rather, we are each a divine spark of the one true living Universe or God. We are the embodied intelligence of the Universe. *I am that. I AM.*

CHAPTER NINE

How Creative Energy Works

From nothing comes everything.
From chaos comes creation.
From creation comes destruction.
From nothing comes everything.

— *CYCLOPEA*

As the embodied god that you are, with your third eye/pineal gland and heart chakra activated, you are now ready to learn how creative energy works.

Everything in the Universe has spin or rotational movement. Everything is in constant motion and flux. In this moment, you are swimming in a vortex of energy. Filaments of the physical precipitate of the Universe spiral around you. From your center of the Universe, your sacred coordinate, an infinite number of vectors can be projected through every plane of existence.

Everything revolves around you. You are the sun/son of God. Your intentions are constantly being projected out from your bundle of Source energy. These projections form a toroid or torus-shaped coil. These coils are used as inductors of electricity causing current to flow. When a magnet is introduced inside a coil, electrical current is produced. In your case, your intention (conscious awareness) creates the coil or electro. Your heart is the magnetic portion. Without feeling (heart energy) behind your intentions, there is no flow of electrons, and no flow of creation is possible. Feeling is the initiatory energy of creation.

Movement or spin is crucial to the development of a toroidal pattern. This pattern acts as a container for the precipitates of your desire. What is happening here is a bending of time and space, matter and light, making it possible for them to be woven into physicality.

FIGURE 31: Image of a Galaxy *(Courtesy of NASA)*

Picture yourself standing inside an inflatable donut-shaped flotation device that is located at the level of your heart. This donut represents a coil of wire. Your body is the magnet, with your head positively charged and your feet negatively charged. This image is mirrored in the images of black holes around which the galaxies rotate.

If you turn the inflatable donut or coil while remaining stationary, electrons will start to flow within the coil. As discussed in Chapter 3, electricity will only flow if the two poles are oppositely charged. In other words, in order for matter to exist, there must be opposites: positive and negative charges. What is interesting about the movement of charge is that it is always toward the positive charge. Also, a system always reverts back to positive energy. A negative energy system is temporary.

The shape of a torus makes it a good subtle energy transducer, meaning it is able to step down higher energy and convert it from one form to another. This form also creates the perfect environment for an infinite number of harmonic energies to travel. The neat thing about this is that as energy is stepped down through this cascade of harmonic frequencies, no energy is lost. Your heart is a dynamic dipole, constantly depolarizing and repolarizing. The heart's torus-shaped electromagnetic field, and the vortex-like shape of the heart itself, provides a perfect staircase from heaven, if you will, through which Source energy flows. Tachyon energy may explain this. Sounds like a term from Star Trek! What affects the flow of this energy is coherence of the particles within your heart, which happens when you feel love in your heart. Love is the key to connecting heaven's USB cable in your heart. I will talk more about love in Chapter 14, Logging into the Heart of Creation.

Tachyons are subatomic particles whose squared mass is negative and that travel faster than the speed of light! There is debate among physicists whether tachyons really exist because they don't fit neatly into some of their current theories. Some mystics say tachyon energy is the same as prana, chi, or universal life force energy. I believe that tachyons are the microcosm of the center of black holes, the smallest "particles" or quanta of zero-point energy.

Your heart brings in Source energy in useable quantities through the coherent property of love. Sounds like a great place from which to start creating!

Coherence within the Heart

Creating coherence within the heart can be accomplished through certain feelings. Positive feelings such as gratitude and compassion produce harmonic heart rhythms or heart coherence (McCraty and Childre 2010, 11-12). The Global Coherence Initiative, which was created by the Institute of HeartMath˚, theorizes that the emotional energy from each of our hearts affects the earth's geomagnetic and magnetic fields and the earth's fields also feedback and affect us. The Global Coherence Initiative takes this theory a step further and postulates that as more people come into heart coherence the more we can positively affect the earth's fields (McCraty and Childre 2010, 21). The Global Coherence Initiative was created to demonstrate the impact of having thousands of people direct positive emotions (heart coherence) toward the common outcomes of peace, balance, and cooperation (http://glcoherence.org).

Remember that we live in a consensus reality. Consensus in this context refers to harmonic group energy. When you as an individual choose to create, group energy is missing. This is why so many books on manifesting don't get readers beyond this point; either the readers' desires don't manifest or take years to manifest. That's because your feelings fuel creation; they don't ignite it. You need a focalizing center of gravitational pull, a vortex of centripetal energy converging to a point. In other words, you need to be creating through a mini black hole or torus. You can do this by using your heart's electromagnetic field.

Sound Waves

Creative energy moves in specific wave formations. These formations are the result of a propagation of harmonic wave patterns. The patterns are the result of coherent resonance of the subatomic particles of matter.

Take for example a piece of clay. It holds a particular wave frequency while it is compressed in a lump. As the clay is molded and shaped, the wave pattern of its subatomic particles changes. Depending on the shape, the particles will form harmonious or disharmonious wave patterns. Shape or form affects the sound or wave propagation of the particles. If the shape is harmonious or "sound," the clay holds its shape. If the shape is disharmonious and coherent wave propagation is not possible, the shape will not last and the clay will revert back to the lump. It is a matter of gravity *and* coherence of the particles.

Inherent in coherence is the conglomeration of particles in the longitudinal sound wave. In these waves, the particles can become compressed. The particles of creation generally move in transverse waves or sine waves. To be able to order the particles, the wave property must change from transverse sine waves to longitudinal/compression sound waves. Ordering up! Isn't that what we are doing when we choose to manifest? We are placing an order with heaven. So, we must "order" the particles of creation to manifest. Sound or words are the maître d' of the Universe. Sound places the order of the particles of creation.

Not just any sound will do. If you choose to order a cheeseburger, you ask for a cheeseburger. You don't ask for a fish sandwich. How, then, do you place a coherent order with the unified field?

First, it is important to realize that all fields throughout the Universe emerge from and flow through the unified field and are in constant dynamic flux, be they magnetic fields, electric fields, electromagnetic fields, gravitational fields, etc. Your order must first resonate and become coherent within your heart's electromagnetic field.

The Sound of Creation

In the beginning was the Word... Words are powerful tools of creation. In his book *Sensitive Chaos: The Creation of Flowing Forms in Water and Air,* Theodor Schwenk writes that everything in nature is given a new energy when it is named. He goes on to say that humans have the power to create through the spoken word (or sound) from which form is created (Schwenk 2008, 131).

According to J. J. Hurtak in *The Keys of Enoch*[*] (Key 305: 9-10) a particular grouping of Hebrew words can align your biorhythms, including your heartbeat, with your higher self. They can also align your mind with the mind of God (Hurtak 1987, 388). Such an alignment is incredibly powerful; it empowers and prepares you for creating. (I will have more to say about divine alignment in Chapter 11.) These words are also used by Jews and Christians alike to honor God. There are several different spellings and pronunciations of these powerful words. The version I like to use is the Hebrew version *Kadosh, Kadosh, Kadosh Adonai Tz'vaot,* which translates as Holy, Holy, Holy is the Lord of Hosts. Hurtak spells it quite differently. Say it aloud now to clear, cleanse, and align your energy with that of Prime Creator.

Now that you have prepared yourself for manifesting, what's next? It is important to remember that we are working with wave propagation of subatomic particles, which affect the wave properties of the heart's electromagnetic field, which in turn affects the unified field. How do you, in effect, travel from field to field to access the precipitate to create physical matter? Come on, think. How is everything in the Universe connected? Yeah, everything is connected through the unified field. But *how* is it connected? Yes! It is all connected through wormholes or portals! Wormholes or portals are like Alice's rabbit hole: They can take you to distant places in the blink of an eye. So the first step in accessing precipitate is to open a portal or connect through God's USB portal.

"And I say unto you, Ask, and it shall be given you; seek, and ye shall find; knock, and it shall be opened unto you" (Luke 11:9 KJV). Knock on the door or, in this case, the portal and it will be opened! After all, the word "portal" means door or gate. So, how do you ask? Where do you knock? The first thing to remember is that Jesus spoke in Aramaic. The second is that he used Aramaic while performing his miracles, so it must be a powerful language. Aramaic for "be opened" is *ephphatha*. Surely not coincidentally, the Egyptian deity, Ptah, was known as the *opener*, the guardian of space and creation who *speaks* the Universe into existence. He was also associated with Archangel Metatron. Remember Metatron's cube? Notice how closely part of the command "phatha" is to Ptah. According to the Bible, Jesus used this command prior to healing.

The Aramaic word closest to the idea of the unified field is *Alaha,* meaning divine oneness, sacred unity, or God. In fact, "Alaha" was used by the Essenes as their word for God. The Hebrew word for God, *Elowah* with its plural form, *Elohim,* derives from Alaha. So one way to open a portal could be by saying *"Alaha, Ephphatha!"* Sounds more like a command of the Universe than a polite request. Indeed. What do gods incarnate do? Command the Universe.

Wunderbar! (No, that's not another command; it is German for "wonderful.") Houston, we have a portal! Now, what?! Bring the subatomic particles into coherence so that they become nonlocal, which means they are suited up, strapped in, and all systems are go for launch. How do we do that, you ask? Remember that sound orders the particles? Good. Now we can place our order with the Universe.

I said earlier that the vibration of love has an inherent coherence. So part of manifesting is to love your desire into existence. You may be thinking I love money and I haven't seen fifties and hundreds show up in my living room. True. That's because it takes more than the feeling of love; it also takes the *sound* of love.

What does love sound like? Love is the harmonic expression of the all and the nothing, of all sound and the ineffable, the finite and the infinite. Great, but what does that mean? The Golden Mean Ratio, or Phi ratio, is said to represent love. This ratio, which has no beginning or end, is seen throughout nature. It is the ultimate expression of the divine. What does the Golden Mean sound like?

Any tones with a ratio between them approximately equal to the Golden Mean, 1.6180339887, will produce the sound. For example, simultaneously striking a 414.2 Hz tuning fork and a 256 Hz tuning fork will produce the Golden Mean Ratio. Do we need tuning forks in order to create? No. Once we have full access to our heart energy, we only need chant the Aramaic word for a radiant love that radiates after opening the pineal gland, and the kind of love that radiates from our enlightened heart once we do our inner work. According to Neil Douglas-Klotz in, *The Hidden Gospel: Decoding the Spiritual Message of the Aramaic Jesus,* that Aramaic word is *rahm* (Douglas-Klotz 2001, 144).

In Chapter 8, we have broken rahm down to its component parts already. Now, we're going to tone it. Notice that as you do you are vibrating your chest and heart with the "ra" sound and your head with the "hm" sound.

TRY IT: Place your left hand over your heart and your right hand on your forehead while you tone "ra-hm." You will feel your heart vibrate to "ra" and your head vibrate to "hm." It is easy to feel how this word naturally harmonizes your mind with your heart. The thought of your desire is now coherent with your feeling of your desire. This heart-mind coherence is crucial for the precipitate to form in the physical. As you tone rahm over and over, you are creating a loop circuit between your heart and your brain. The energy oscillates between the two.

Notice that the circuit starts in your heart and then goes to the brain. As I have said before, the heart, not the brain, is mission control. The electromagnetic field of the heart causes the electromagnetic field of the brain to harmonize with it. Once these fields harmonize, they form a common dipole moment, which produces a portal through which the precipitate can emerge.

According to Tom Bearden, whose work is based in part on a 1903 paper by E. T. Whittaker, a dipole can produce pairs of longitudinal (in this case, scalar) electromagnetic waves that emanate in two directions (Bearden 2000, 2 and Whittaker 1903). If you recall, Tesla purported that scalar waves are longitudinal waves. If scalar waves were transverse and not longitudinal, then we could not enter the ongoing moment of creation through scalar technology and be the co-creators that we are.

Repeating rahm sets up an oscillation of energy between the electromagnetic field of the heart and the electromagnetic field of the brain. This oscillation of longitudinal scalar waves creates Bearden's negentropy or Tesla's free energy generator. Remember the Gregg Braden quote in Chapter 5 about the heart being a liquid crystal oscillator? Here is another level of oscillation with the heart.

Having opened a portal, we must close it when we are finished. This is done by bringing your hands together in prayer position in front of your heart and saying, "It is done!" This seals the energy and closes the portal.

The final step is to thank the Universe for having answered your request and to feel gratitude in your heart. Gratitude is a powerful emotion that ensures flow from Source. Any questions? I bet. Don't worry. We'll go over this in more detail in Chapter 13, Stairway to Heaven. But first, let's talk more about where precipitation comes from, and I don't mean the kind that falls from the sky. Precipitate does not come into physical form in drips and drabs, or drops like rain for that matter. It manifests through etheric templates.

CHAPTER TEN

Blueprints of Creation

*Every well built house started in the form of a **definite purpose***
plus a definite plan in the nature of a set of blueprints.

— ***NAPOLEON HILL*** *– THE LAW OF SUCCESS: THE 16 SECRETS*
FOR ACHIEVING WEALTH & PROSPERITY

In her interview with Dr. Hal Putoff, Lynne McTaggart writes in, *The Field: The Quest for the Secret Force of the Universe,* that Putoff had wondered if the zero-point field could act as a sort of blueprint or grid through which coherent energy or matter could be imparted (McTaggart 2002, 35). I call these "blueprints of creation" from a holographic slice of the unified field, etheric templates.

You sketched the blueprint for your life prior to birth. From this blank matrix or template, you chose what to work on in this lifetime – you co-authored with Source your sacred contract, as Caroline Myss calls it. Once the contract was signed, preformed etheric templates, as I refer to them, formed for each of the major cycles in your life. These templates ensure you will fulfill your contract. They chart your destiny.

When people ask me whether we have free will or if life is predetermined, the answer I give is yes and no. We have free will at the soul level when we co-create our contract for this life. Once we sign on the line, our life is mapped out. The highways of our life's journey are determined before we embody. However, once embodied, we can choose to take as many side streets as we like on the way to our ultimate destination.

Think of your preformed etheric templates as a pre-manufactured house. The kit dimensions are already determined and you choose the color of the walls, appliances, furniture, etc. Once you make these decisions, the house is finished and ready to move in. Similarly, these templates are not complete without some pivotal choices on our part. Without them, we cannot bring our template into the physical. We use the term "at a cross-roads" when we know we must make an important decision. Crossroads can be challenging until we understand what is really happening. At these points in our lives, we are usually asked to go deeper into trust and to sur-render – to *our* divine plan. When we realize that we are not placing blind trust in something outside of ourselves but rather trusting what our higher or essential selves mapped for us in this life, we can let go of attachments and face our fear. We free-fall into our own arms, knowing that our divine nature is always there to catch us.

The phrase "at a crossroads" fits quite well in my highway analogy, since it signals that it is time to take a different highway. The term *cross*roads also refers to the sacred coordinate in our heart and to the journey into our heart, where we choose and create the final touches for the etheric templates that are the precursors to manifesting our heart's desire.

Etheric Templates

As stated earlier, etheric templates are newly created etheric fractals of the unified field. Ether is the first precipitate to form, even before atoms come together. Although ether cannot be seen, the effects of ether can be meas-ured and observed. Ether is the backdrop for all matter, the canvas upon which you, as a co-creator, paint your desires.

Once the etheric template is created, the blueprint energy of your desire is held, just as if you had saved the information on a hard drive. The infor-mation remains there until it is erased. While in this form, the information is not physical, in the sense that it cannot be seen by the naked eye or touched with your hands; however, it can be felt by your heart, since it is held in your heart field.

An etheric template is a holographic representation of your desire. It is as if by beaming your thought through the projector of your mind, you create the image on a computer screen. Since the Universe is one big mir-ror, what is projected in your mind is reflected out into the unified field accordingly. The phrase "put it out there" becomes literal, and the notion of "projecting thought forms" also takes on a new meaning! Since it is "out there," others can tap into the template, too.

In *The Masters and the Spiritual Path,* the Prophets add that a template of an idea in your mind is also held out there and, because of this, other people may tune into that idea and claim it as their own (Prophet 2001, 51).

Manifesting Using Preformed Templates

Scalar waves form the template for the precipitate of matter. The heart field informs the scalar waves; hence the energy or vibration of the heart field dictates the final form. As the template vibrates to the frequency of the information, charged particles are released. This buildup of charge provides the energy needed to move and align the precipitate on the template. Once the particles are in place on the template, their dipoles align and discharge any excess charge, thus stopping the formation of the template. This creates the preformed etheric template.

Your next question is probably, "How do I bring the etheric template into physical manifestation?" The template, as is everything else in the Universe, is vibrating. If you remember from my translation equation on page 70, tension, or *intention*, slows the particles. Tension is a pulling force exerted by one object on another object. Your *in-tension* is literally pulling on the etheric template and bringing it down into the physical. Gregg Braden refers to magnetic tension as the "glue of consciousness" (Braden 1997, 21). Remember, though, that the template is made of ether, not of subatomic or atomic particles. These particles of matter are not yet in order on the template.

Placing your "order" is nothing more than placing your attention on your desired outcome. The attention that is required here is the sound of "ah," which happens to be the heart chakra sound! Remember "Alaha, Ephphatha?" Which vowel sound do you hear most when you say these words? Not only is the "ah" sound opening the portal to bring down the etheric template, you are placing your "ah-tension" from your heart onto your heart's desire. This focused energy acts like a laser beam to concentrate the movement of particles into the etheric blueprint. The origin of this "ah-tension" is your sacred coordinate. It is from this point that the tracker beam of your heart shines its light to guide in the particles. Think of it as the ground crew that guides the plane into the gate.

To precipitate your template, it is essential to be in resonance with the frequency of your desired manifestation. This requires feeling what it feels like for you to already have whatever it is you choose to manifest. Holding this feeling in your heart and allowing it to permeate your whole body creates an electrical potential or charge throughout the body. Water, which responds to emotions, becomes like an antenna that sends the signal to the Universe, saying, "Place the precipitate here." Without creating this potential – literally the potential to be, to do, or have whatever we desire – the precipitate is lost and the template not grounded.

Resonating at the frequency of enthusiasm for your desired creation ensures its manifestation. The word "enthusiasm" comes from the Greek word *enthousiamos,* meaning having a god within or inspired from God. The god that you are commands from the frequency of enthusiasm!

Once we reach that frequency of enthusiasm, our entire being becomes magnetic. The magnetic field around the heart with the unified field, align, transforming the body into a dipole. Not only are your electromagnetic fields then aligned, but the water within you becomes a coherent dipole. We become the dipole moment, super-radiant, and magnetic. Is this what it means to have a magnetic personality?!

Etheric Templates and the Ascension Process

During this time of ascension, the changes in Earth's electromagnetic field, its rotation, and the sun are crucial for accelerating the change within our quantum field. The combination of the increase in charged particles and photons coming from the sun with the decrease in the earth's magnetic field defenses creates the perfect environment to overload our circuitry. This huge influx of light/information causes the brain's neurons to "light up." Because the brain cannot assimilate this huge volume of information, what happens next is a "brain dump." Instead of short-circuiting, the brain dumps its information into the heart, which has had control of the brain all along. Since the brain's waves are harmonized to the heart's waves, this makes for a smooth transfer of information.

Once the transfer is complete, the heart literally overflows with energy and information and the overflow, "my cup runneth over," moves *up* to the high heart. The high heart then becomes the clearing house for information and life choices. We can no longer be concerned with third-dimensional thoughts since our awareness has now shifted to fourth-dimensional awareness. It is as if you had been seeing the world from a snail's perspective and can now see it through the eyes of an eagle. In a nutshell, this is how we are becoming "enlightened."

Entering Fourth-and Fifth-Dimensional Awareness

The opening of the high heart naturally occurs with this large influx of energy. As the energy moves into the high heart, some people may find themselves feeling overwhelmed with light, color, symbols, words, sounds, energy rush, emotions, and/or other information.

If you are one of them, the best technique to clear the feeling of overwhelm from your mind is to breathe deeply and smile as you breathe, remaining focused on your heart as you feel it filling up. It may help to place your hand over your heart while you ride the waves of energy as they come in. Once the heart is full, you may feel as though you cannot catch your breath, but this will last for only a second. Once the energy shifts, you will feel your consciousness expand. You will soon feel heat at the crown chakra because the influx of light has opened your crown chakra. Remain seated or lie down to allow the integration of this energy until you feel centered and sense that the process is complete.

Now, the vibratory frequency of your particles matches that of the particles within the etheric template. Through the ascension process, you are able to manipulate matter. You can see your etheric templates with your third eye, whether they are the ones you formed prior to birth or later with your thoughts. By thinking of and feeling the effect of your desire, you will create all or part of the template. Your thoughts become magnetized and create tiny magnetic fields that literally attract the etheric template to you.

Since ether has a negative mass and density, your thoughts are also attracting particles and arranging them to form electrons and protons, atoms and molecules. This is the power of your thoughts. The time it takes to bond the particles into a physical object decreases as you learn how to train your thoughts. In fourth-dimensional awareness, we manipulate the ether through thought forms. We "in-form" the particles, which, in turn, form the template.

As your conscious expands into fifth-dimensional awareness, you will be able to precipitate the template – in other words, manifest your desire – instantaneously. This is why ascension is a process. Can you imagine what this world would be like if you were able to immediately manifest your thoughts without accessing higher consciousness through your heart?

The Universe is on purpose. There is a reason and a physical law that dictates the behavior of all of creation. Now that the connection to particle heaven is open and the particles know to which template to go, the next instruction is where to align on the template.

CHAPTER ELEVEN

Aligning with the Divine

When you make the two one, and when you make the inside
like the outside and the outside like the inside, and the above
like the below, and when you make the male and female one and
the same, so that the male not be male nor the female female;
and when you fashion eyes in the place of an eye, and a hand
in place of a hand, and a foot in place of a foot, and a likeness
in place of a likeness; then you will enter [the kingdom].

— *THE GOSPEL OF THOMAS, SAYING 22*
TRANSLATION EDITED BY JAMES MCCONLEY ROBINSON

Power comes with alignment, whether it is aligning your will with divine will or the aligning of electromagnetic fields, dipoles, or precipitate on an etheric template. Alignment is like inserting a key into a lock – it opens doorways of possibilities.

Aligning our desires with that of the Universe ensures their manifestation. In *Love Without End - Jesus Speaks,* Glenda Green writes that it is through the stillness of the heart that we obtain higher knowledge, and it is within the heart that we align our will with the will of God (Green 2002, 136). The moment we align our will with God's will, magic happens.

The true manifestation of your life's purpose occurs once the inner you matches the outer you. In other words, you become congruent at all levels, especially at the subtle energy levels of aligning your thought patterns with your original divine blueprint. You cannot be congruent if you believe you are one thing and act as though you are another. Incongruity is the mother of discontent. First align your thoughts and behaviors with who you really are. Then things will line up in your life.

Part of the magic of congruency is that once you tune into the atomic blueprint of a thing and align your consciousness with it, you become part of it. In *Masters and the Spiritual Path,* the Prophets write that it is through congruency that you are able to overcome the physical limitations of matter (Prophet 2001, 294).

In order to be congruent, the masculine and feminine energies within each of us must be balanced. The marriage of opposites within is the nature of the divine. The primary force of creation lies within us, not outside of us. This balance point simulates the zero-point energy field and aligns it with your divine blueprint, thus manifesting your divine plan. The Gospel of Thomas, Saying 106 states: *"Jesus said, 'When you make the two into one, you will become children of Adam,' and when you say, 'Mountain, move from here!' it will move"* (Miller 1994, 321). You will find techniques to balance the masculine and feminine energies in Chapter 12.

Levels of Alignment

When we align our will with divine will, every aspect of our multi-dimensional selves aligns. At the macrocosmic level, the sacred coordinate within our hearts, the sun that we are, aligns with the sun in our solar system, which aligns with the galactic center, which aligns with the Great Central Sun. The sacred coordinate within our hearts also aligns with our sacred coordinate on the divine matrix or unified field. In other words, we are

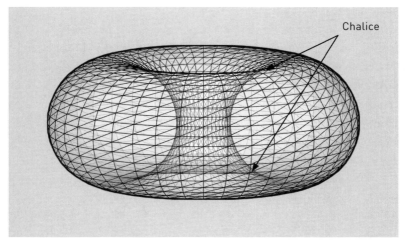

Chalice

FIGURE 32: How Information Aligns in the Body

receiving information in our hearts from the divine intelligence through our cosmic self. We are directly connected to Source energy, as though we are hardwired to a cosmic computer. This is how we align our will with divine will. We become the vessel through which the information flows. The center of the torus-shaped Universe looks like a chalice. The chalice within the torus of our hearts is the chalice of divine will that is manifested in the physical.

The heart is a vessel for information. Information or light comes to us from the unified field through the connection from the sacred coordinate within our heart. Information processing always starts within the heart. As explained in Chapter 5, the light received from the black-white whole within the heart is transported via the water in the blood throughout the body.

This Magic Dipole Moment

We are electromagnetic beings living in a sea of electromagnetic fields while the unified field flows through us and through every other field. This web of electromagnetism is constantly sending and receiving information through each field. Our vibrational frequency attunes us to the fields in the same way you might tune into a radio station. The higher your frequency, the more "stations" or fields you are able to tune into. How do you tune into a particular field of information?

Have you ever wondered why water makes up the majority of our bodies and of the earth? Water, being a polar molecule, and because of its unique ability to form hydrogen bonds with itself, is able to deftly align its polar heads and structure itself while in liquid form. Liquid crystal molecules within liquids have the ability to structure themselves like water. Phospholipids in the cell membrane and cholesterol are two such liquid crystal molecules. These liquid crystals act like radio tuners for our body. Their unique propensity to align is also vital to the flow of information.

Information (energy) will flow if there is a pathway through which it can move. Alignment of molecules, or a dipole moment, creates a pathway. Think of this pathway as the yellow brick road that Dorothy followed in *The Wizard of Oz*. Without each brick in its proper place, there would be no easy path for her to follow and no discernible yellow brick road. Similarly, dipole water molecules line up to form a pathway or "USB cable" through

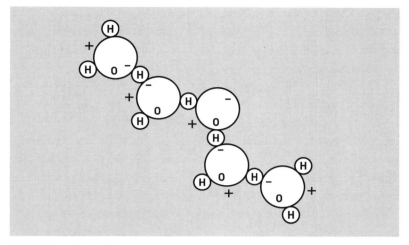

FIGURE 33: Dipole Moment of Water Molecules

which information can flow. Liquid crystals respond to electromagnetic fields and align based on that field. So, to which field do the liquid crystals in your body respond? Your heart field, of course!

As I have previously stated in Chapter 6, according to Gregg Braden, compassion (or come-passion, as I like to write it), is how the liquid crystals within the cells align with the heart (Braden 1997, 156). When we live with passion and ignite the fire within our hearts, we ignite our ability to manifest.

Your heart's desire or *in*tention creates an electromagnetic field by aligning the dipole water molecules within your body. Remember that highly aligned water molecules become superconductive with no electrical resistance. When dipoles align, they open the door through which etheric templates descend. This superconductive field magnetically draws the etheric template to align itself with this field.

The etheric template resonates at the same frequency as the superconductive dipole field and the two become coherent, entrained, and indistinguishable. In *Sensitive Chaos*, Schwenk uses the term "etheric forces" to describe how matter is formed. He goes on to say that these "etheric forces" use water as the medium through which information is transferred to the physical through resonance between water and these forces (Schwenk 2008, 95). It is as though the dipole water moments create small peg holes within the template into which atoms instantaneously arrange themselves. Once all of the peg holes are filled, the desire is precipitated. It is interesting that the word "precipitate" is used for manifesting and also for water that falls as rain, snow, or sleet.

Dipoles are like tumblers on a lock. Once all are aligned to that particular lock or pathway, doors open – or rather – portals. Yes, portals.

At the heart of everything is opposites, or, in this case, a dipole. According to Thomas Bearden, these dipoles produce longitudinal scalar electromagnetic waves that are capable of spreading energy in all directions. The dipole takes energy out of the field and orders the electromagnetic waves from the field producing what he calls "negentropy," (Bearden 2000, 1,4,7). When the liquid crystals (water) within our body create a dipole moment, they align or order our energy like soldiers in formation. These dipole moments may create the portals through which we are able to access other dimensions.

As Earth shifts her poles, the polarities within us also shift. These dipole moments become increasingly important as on-off switches that open the flow of information from electromagnetic fields that, up until now, have been inaccessible. The influx of high frequency energy during the shift is our access pass to worlds once unknown.

Every electromagnetic field generated by a human heart is harmonized with the earth's electromagnetic field. As the magnetic field of the earth approaches zero and as magnetic north keeps shifting, our hearts' fields are constantly changing in response to the earth's magnetic field changes. In addition, our heart field is in communication with every other heart field.

Memory/information is held in magnetic fields. Think of Earth's process of decreasing magnetic-field strength as "letting our guards down." The earth opens her door through which more information can flow as we become more open to receiving it. Since we live in a holographic Universe, every planet, star, and galaxy is experiencing a similar phenomenon. Add the photon belt and the Great Central Sun to this increased influx of charged particles from our sun, and you have a recipe for high speed mega download!

Remember that information flows both ways – not only are we being informed by Earth and the unified field, we are also informing Earth and the field. Without this feedback loop, the field would not receive the necessary information to effectively regulate the influx of information through our hearts. As I pointed out in Chapter 2, the torus shape of the "great" black-white whole is self-reflexive. The shape of a torus suggests that energy or information flows in and out. The Universe doesn't have any secrets. It shares all it knows with all that is; hence, information is constantly renewed and advanced.

As the magnetic field of the earth decreases, our ability to manifest increases. Particle alignment within etheric templates is more precise with less outside magnetic interference, and the templates precipitate faster. There is more information to fill the form of etheric templates at the same time as there is less magnetic resistance to flow. Sounds like a co-creator's dream!

Remember our prime creation triangle, figure 9 in Chapter 3? Creative energy only flows when there are opposites, i.e. positive and negative charge. This energy flows because there is a *pathway* through which it can flow. The pathway is initiated through positive and negative charges connecting and becoming one or neutral. Neutrality is dynamic; there is no build up of charge since free flow is allowed. The goal of all systems is a state of neutrality or equilibrium. Creation comes when we align ourselves with the flow – of creative particles, etheric templates, and electromagnetic fields.

Everything changes when you see the world with new eyes. You are able to access more dimensions than you did before. Seeing departed loved ones, conversing with extraterrestrial intelligences, and feeling the emotions of others becomes an everyday occurrence. Science takes a quantum leap and new theories make old ones look like kindergarten material. When you are aligned with the divine, you live as the god that you are.

Alignment is aligning the whole with the holes of creation. Right relationship yields this alignment. When you bring the inner you to the outer and live as the god that you are, you are in alignment with creation. Divine consciousness wills divine consciousness for its creation. *"Thy will be done on earth as it is in heaven"* (The Lord's Prayer). There is no separation at any level of consciousness. It is all a matter of aligning your will with divine will.

The universal mind knows only love. When you awaken to the truth that all is one and all is love, you are in complete alignment. At that point, interestingly, the word "alignment" loses its meaning. When you realize that all is one, there can be no misalignment, for alignment implies that at least two things must come together. Before you can manifest, you must first come to this realization, that all is one, that everything that has, is, and will be already exists within the unified field. All you are doing is manipulating form. What you create is not outside yourself. It is merely an aspect of you since you are part of the unified field. Manipulate the field within your heart and the unified field will spontaneously generate your desire. This is at-one-ment.

Every crafter or creator has tools of the trade. Now that you know all the fundamentals of creating, the next chapter will provide you, the novice creator, with a useful set of tools for your new trade.

CHAPTER TWELVE

Tools for Creation

A true creator creates with one hand
in Earth and the other in Heaven.

– *CYCLOPEA*

I have chosen the ankh as a simple yet powerful tool to assist you in living as the co-creator that you are. The ankh was used by the ancient Egyptians. It has also been referred to as the Egyptian crux ansata or looped tau-cross. It is shaped like the human body, and in some of the meditations that follow, you can use your body in place of the ankh.

The ankh is a symbol of eternal life and was known as the key of life to the Egyptians. To them, the key to life lay in reconciling opposites – balancing the masculine active energy with the feminine passive energy. It even looks like a key. The ankh is also a fertility symbol, with the loop representing the womb and the vertical line representing the phallus. Whenever the magnetic feminine energies are in contact with the electric masculine

FIGURE 34: Egyptian Ankh

energies, energy flows, and whenever opposites dance together, creation happens.

The ankh can be used as a symbol for many things. In Chapter 8, we talked about the energy flow from the lower dantian, through the middle dantian, to the upper dantian (pineal gland), and then back down to the heart. You can use the ankh as a tool to follow the flow of this energy: It starts up the shaft of the ankh (sacral chakra), through the cross area (heart), and through the loop back to the cross area (from the heart to the pineal gland and back to the heart). The loop of the ankh also symbolizes the glow or halo around the head after the pineal is activated.

Ancient Egyptians believed that the heart was part of the soul and, as such, looked at the heart as the key to the afterlife. They placed great importance on the physical heart being light in weight after death. If the heart of the deceased weighed more than the feather of Maat (measured during their Weighing of the Heart ceremony), the monster Ammit ate it immediately. (It is interesting that the word "light" can refer to weight or the electromagnetic spectrum.) The terms "light-hearted" and "light as a feather" emerged from these Egyptian practices. Also, "Joy resides in the heart" is one of my nine keys in *In the Key of Life* (Cerio 2007, 46). According to the ancient Egyptians, when you live your life light-heartedly, full of joy, and full of light, you hold the key to eternal life.

The Ankh as a Tool for Balance

One interpretation of the ankh is that it represents the ideal human. The right arm of the ankh represents positive charge, masculine energy, the material, and the physical body. The left arm represents negative charge, feminine energy, antimatter, and the soul. The lower shaft represents the union of positive and negative, masculine and feminine; the loop serves to harmonize the whole.

If we look at the ankh as a symbol for the human body, we can use it as a tool to move excess or charged energy through our bodies. Whenever we become emotionally "charged" about an event, we actually build up an energetic charge in the form of charged particles. The key to emotional balance is to discharge that buildup of charge.

We cannot create from a place of emotional imbalance because it affects our heart's electromagnetic field. If you recall in Chapter 11, you learned that we are swimming in electromagnetic fields and that we are part of the unified field. Electromagnetic fields interact with each other, causing drain or gain depending on the initial state of the field. Therefore, if you start from a deficit when you encounter a "draining" situation, your field will become weaker. Even if you start with an excess when you encounter a draining situation, you will still be drained but not as much. The only way to maintain balance is to "run the energy." Balance is a dynamic state, an ever-changing dance as our frequencies lift higher and higher as we dissipate our emotional charge.

I am not suggesting that you not allow yourself to feel your emotions. The body has a clever way of taking on unexpressed emotional energy and hiding it deep within. The neurotransmitters that produce the feeling of emotions only remain in the blood for ninety seconds, which means that if you stay in the emotion past ninety seconds, your brain sets up a loop and reruns the emotion. As you can imagine, this is not healthy. I suggest that you allow yourself to fully feel the emotion for ninety seconds. Time it if you can. At the end of the ninety seconds, run the energy using the ankh tool as described below.

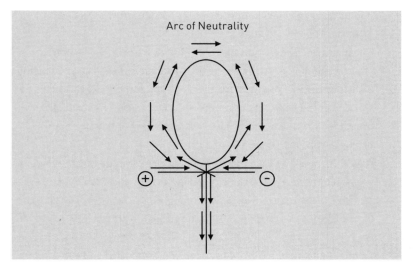

FIGURE 35: Ankh with arrows depicting flow of energy coming in from left and right, through the heart, looping through the arc of neutrality, then back through the heart, and into the ground.

Figure 35 shows how to use the ankh to mirror your body and direct the energy to attain and maintain emotional balance. Whenever you feel out of sorts, out of balance, or really charged about something, use the following technique to balance your energy.

Meditation for Dissipating and Balancing Energy

Imagine and feel the flow of energy in your own body or, if you like, use an ankh as a surrogate for yourself. Hold it in your hand and visualize the movement of energy through the ankh as I describe below.

1. Stand with your feet shoulder width apart, arms out at your sides, and with your palms facing up.
2. As you inhale, imagine feminine energy entering your left palm and continuing through your left arm to your heart. Feminine energy (yin) includes allowing, receiving, nurturing, passivity, intuiting, unconditional love, and creative imagination.
3. At the right palm, imagine masculine energy entering and traveling through your right arm into your heart, where it meets and crosses at the sacred coordinate and continues up into the brain. Masculine energy (yang) includes acting, giving, inner strength, courage, and rational left brain activities.
4. The masculine energy now enters the left hemisphere of the brain while the feminine energy enters the right hemisphere, each of which is their respective homes, since each hemisphere controls the opposite side of the body. As the energy continues to the crown, hold your breath for a moment and visualize the two energies crossing paths, producing an arc of neutrality.
5. As the energies continue through the brain and into the heart (where they become balanced) exhale, expelling all the air in your lungs as you visualize the energy moving down through your spine, through your legs, into your feet, and finally into the ground to literally ground the energy.
6. Continue the meditation until you feel more balanced and at peace.

Remember that you must align yourself with the divine in order to create. This means balancing the divine feminine and masculine within. In addition, using the ankh as a tool for balance and dissipating excess energy clears your aura or bio-field of static, similar to the static on a radio when the signal is weak. It is important to create from a static-free grounded energy. Once you instill a state of balance, you can use the ankh as a tool to increase your energy to prepare you for manifesting.

Meditation for Enhancing Energy

The ankh can also be used to increase your heart's electromagnetic field. Charging your heart's field enhances your ability to command the particles of creation. In this meditation, you will use the ankh as a capacitor instead of a dissipater of energy. Instead of allowing the energy to ground into the earth, you will concentrate it in your heart chakra and your heart's electromagnetic field. In this way, the ankh can provide the "capacity" to create. It takes energy to move energy and, by doing the following meditation, you will recharge your batteries.

1. Begin by focusing on your sacred coordinate through which creative energy flows. Imagine it is filled with brilliant golden light.
2. Next, chant "ra." Ra is the name of the ancient Egyptian sun god.
3. While keeping your attention in your heart, imagine energy coming from above and below you, and from your left and right, then meeting in your heart. By doing this, you are using the cross of the sacred coordinate, or in this case, the ankh. The energy that comes from above and below you mostly flows through what is called the prana tube. Prana is another name for life force energy. This tube extends through the perineum to one hand length below the feet and through the pineal gland to one hand length above the head.
4. While you are imagining the energy entering from above your head, as it enters the pineal gland, imagine that it bifurcates, taking two side trips through the right and left hemispheres of the brain. (Imagining the energy flowing through each hemisphere of the brain before entering the heart ensures a balanced mind and heart.)
5. Now, imagine that the energy rejoins within the prana tube at the high heart and travels to the heart.
6. Return your focus to your arms. Imagine the energy coming from your right and left arms, first flowing through each of your palm chakras,

then through each arm, and into your heart. (The palm chakra is an extension of the heart chakra.)

7. As all of the energies from above and below, left and right, merge within the heart, chant "om." There is no coincidence that the sound of the Universe, "om," has the same pronunciation and nearly the same spelling as the word "ohm," which refers to the measure for capacitance in physics.

8. As you chant "om," feel the energy build in your heart and imagine your sacred coordinate getting brighter and brighter. Allow the energy to permeate your heart field.

Repeat the entire process until you feel it is complete or until you notice an increase in energy in your heart field. Using this technique before practicing the Sacred Coordinate Meditation below facilitates its effects.

Sacred Coordinate Meditation

Your sacred coordinate is your connection with Source. When you are connected to Source energy and vibrating at its frequency, the frequency of love, you are able to entrain the particles of creation. One way to increase and maintain your frequency to that of love is to do the Sacred Coordinate Meditation daily. (You can refer to Fig.2)

1. Sit with your spine straight and take several slow deep breaths.

2. Bring your attention to your physical heart. Feel, don't think, gratitude for your heart, for all of the marvelous work it has done and continues to do for you. Feel gratitude for your connection to Source and the divine within. Keep feeling gratitude until you feel energy moving near or in your heart. You may feel it move into your heart chakra.

3. Allow this energy to expand and enhance your heart chakra and then your heart's electromagnetic field. Take a moment to sense your field and feel gratitude.

4. Now, with your intention, enter the sacred coordinate within your heart. It is between the physical and the nonphysical since you are entering scalar territory, the connecting point to all of creation. It may be easier to imagine you are inside the sacred coordinate of your physical heart. See and feel yourself within this sacred place.

5. Shortly after entering the sacred coordinate, you should feel the emotion of bliss begin to permeate your body and bio-field.

6. Visualize golden light pouring out of your sacred coordinate. This light expands until you are enveloped in gold light like a golden mandorla around your body. Feel the love that is emitted by this golden light.

7. Focus on your heart and feel the holographic image of your sacred coordinate projected on your heart's electromagnetic field. Allow the emotion of bliss to fill each of your atoms, cells, organs, tissues, body, and bio-field. Bask in this bliss for as long as you can.

Repeat this meditation daily until you maintain this blissful feeling or until you feel that this frequency is embedded within your heart field. You have now opened the portal to your heart's desire.

Using the Tools of the Trade

It is important to use each of the above techniques to prepare your energy for creating. Use the ankh to dissipate energy daily or whenever you feel a buildup of charge. It is also a good idea to use it just prior to following the steps of creation delineated in Chapter 13. Similarly, use the ankh to increase your energy and perform the Sacred Coordinate Meditation daily and just prior to creating.

It is also important to keep your energy and your home clear. Smudging, toning, using a rattle, and saying prayers are all good ways to clear the energy. A cluttered energy field slows and may even block the process of creation.

Are you ready to climb the stairway to heaven and create? Good. Then turn the page and read on!

CHAPTER THIRTEEN

Stairway to Heaven

Then answered Jesus and said unto them, Verily, verily,
I say unto you, The Son can do nothing of himself,
but what he sees the Father do: for whatsoever things he does,
these also does the Son likewise.

— JOHN 5:19, KJV

This verse is a beautiful expression of the holographic nature of the Universe. Whatever we see in nature, we are that. We are infinite space, indescribable beauty, unlimited potential, boundless love, almighty power, overflowing joy, endless peace, and embodied truth. We are all of these things because Source energy flows through us. It is this connection to Source that sustains us and is the cause of all things.

When we allow the intelligence of the Universe to guide our lives, we become co-creators. We are able to manifest our desires as long as those desires are in alignment with the universal mind. There are three important keys to remember before you can create as the god that you are.

The first key is to locate your "home base" in the unified field. That's easy to do: Your name signifies your home base. Why is this important? You need a reference point from which to coordinate your creative energy. You are coordinating light and matter, time and space. It is imperative that you know where to bring the energy and that the Universe knows who is commanding it.

The energy of manifestation precipitates through your unique orientation on the grid – your sacred coordinate, God's USB port, that connects with your unique URL on the matrix. You must find your coordinates by stating your name prior to any command. Unlike earthly authorities, the Universe only needs your name for identification; it has no need for fingerprints or passport.

The second key is to follow the law of the mutually exclusive common denominator. "Mutually exclusive common denominator" sounds like an oxymoron, but it's not. You are a conscious co-creator. You are creating with every other multi-dimensional being everywhere at once. Everything that is created is a mutual undertaking. However, it is also exclusive because it is *your* particular energy and coordinates in the matrix that are initializing and initiating your specific creation. What is the common denominator? There is a safety valve within this system that makes certain if your desire for this manifestation is not in harmony with enough of the surrounding energies or with the whole energy, it will not manifest. For example, if you choose to manifest a snowstorm in July in Detroit, that may not be in harmony with the surrounding energies. Therefore, it will not manifest.

The third key is to manifest with love in your heart. The divine masculine and feminine, the electro and the magnetic, are combined and harmonized with the energy of the immaculate conception of your desire. This marriage of polarities fuels the energy for creation. It is as if you are producing a current of creative electricity from the coil of masculine energy and the magnet of feminine energy. Your heart becomes an electrical generator with love fueling its core and your heart's electromagnetic field radiates love – the greatest power in the Universe.

Going with the Flow of Creation

You are a great and powerful being, whose creational energy is waiting to be tapped. Bring forth your firmament of ideas and those cherished wishes that are known to you alone. These desires must bear fruit, for you have sewn them into the hem of your life's garment. In other words, be careful what you wish for, for it will indeed come to pass.

Embody and see your desires as a presence of presents or gifts, if you will; and indeed, it is by your will that you birth them into existence. Your creations are gifts to glorify the goodness and love of the One Source of All. When you create from your heart, you manifest more than your heart's desire. You manifest love for *your* creator.

There are six things that will assist your flow of creation. First, see yourself as a source of abundance. Abundance cannot exist outside of you, since the Universe flows through you. Call upon your stash of cash, your plethora of plenty, and invoke your I AM presence.

Second, you are a part of the universal symphony of creation. You have your own instrument and tone to add to the world. Play it and play with it! Play! Why do you think the word "play" is used to describe how you create music from an instrument? You *play* it. Play and joy are synonymous. As you play while you create, you play your unique instrument and tone for the Universe and you create coherence or harmonic waves of particles. Play and joy serve to accelerate the particles of creation.

Third, place your attention on *all* your thoughts, not just those linked to what it is you wish to create. Focus on thoughts that are in alignment with your heart's desire. But also be aware of any thoughts that are detrimental to creating your wish. When you notice them, make a conscious choice to think them no more. Should a thought come up, visualize yourself erasing it from the whiteboard of your mind. Give it no more energy than this. Remember: Where attention goes, energy flows. Once you have cleared your mind of thoughts that may hamper your creative flow, you can begin to focus your attention.

Attention is merely the flow of electrons towards a source. It requires work to create the flow. If there is no potential gradient, electrons remain in a semi-static state, meaning they can move freely fueled by their own inherent energy but cannot move from or towards something, as they do in a wire once a switch is turned on. This inherent movement is erratic. Applying energy in the form of thought or attention provides the open switch needed to produce a coherent flow of electrons.

Fourth, you cannot manifest that which is not in alignment with your original divine blueprint. You have free will to choose at the level of the conscious mind, but it is the unconscious mind, the universal consciousness, that will always dictate the final outcome. Your subconscious mind was collaboratively preprogrammed by your higher consciousness and the cosmic mind before your embodiment. Your desires are always weighed against your higher needs. Whatever thoughts you have about your thoughts are the most powerful thoughts. This is your higher self talking to you. If your request is in alignment with your original divine blueprint for this lifetime, it will manifest.

Fifth, keep an open mind and heart. Be open to subtle changes, course corrections, and surprises. The universal mind is bigger than your conscious mind and may have a clearer, more effective or more encompassing outcome than your conscious mind could think of to express.

Last, believe the manifestation has already occurred and feel it in your heart. Now, step aside, and allow the flow of creation to move through you and your heart field.

It is important to practice these techniques until you feel you have mastered them *before* ascending creation's staircase as described in the next section. Downloading your divinity is a process that requires dedication.

The Steps to Heaven

After mastering the six ways to stay in the flow of your creation, and using the tools for creation in Chapter 12, you are ready to step into your role as co-creator. In Chapter 9, I described the science behind the steps of creation. For ease of use, here is a list of the verbal steps.

STEP 1
Say out loud, *Kadosh, Kadosh, Kadosh Adonai Tz'vaot* to prepare the energy around you for creation. Holy, holy, holy are you and the Universe indeed!

STEP 2
Say your name out loud to identify your sacred coordinate to the Universe.

STEP 3
Say *Alaha, Ephphatha!* This opens a portal through which the etheric template can move.

STEP 4
State your desire using powerful language. The most powerful way of saying anything is to first say "I AM." When you invoke your "I AM" presence, you are invoking your god self. Here is an example of how to powerfully phrase your desire, "I AM with my ideal partner now."

STEP 5
Chant *rahm*. Remember that rahm means radiant love. Focus on the sacred coordinate in your heart and visualize golden light radiating from it as you chant. Notice that this sounds similar to the chants used in the meditation

for using the ankh as a tool for enhancing energy in Chapter 12. As you chant, feel in your heart what it feels like to already have your desire with you now. Visualize your heart's desire. Remember that chanting rahm sets up an electromagnetic oscillation between your heart and brain, linking the energy of the thought of your creation with your sacred coordinate and your heart field. Continue chanting until it feels complete.

Step 6

Say "It is done." As you say this, bring your palms together in prayer position in front of your heart to seal the energy and close the portal.

Step 7

Thank the Universe for what has already been manifested and feel gratitude in your heart.

Your work is complete. Trust that the Universe has heard your command and is responding. As the frequency of your body increases, the time between your command and its physical manifestation will decrease. Eventually, you will be able to focus your thoughts with such laser precision, and radiate such love and light from your heart, that your desire will manifest instantaneously.

Once freed, the heart knows no limits. It creates unceasingly, doing the bidding of your god self. The phrase, *"As I think, so I am,"* is true, but only after your thoughts pass through your sacred coordinate – your USB port to the divine.

Without the unified field as our Source, we could do nothing. Everything comes from this eternal enigma; the one and the many, the all and the nothing, the knowable and the unknowable.

CHAPTER FOURTEEN

Logging into the Heart of Creation

What the mind cannot comprehend,
the heart already knows.

— *CYCLOPEA*

What makes the unified field such an enigma? What is the force behind creation? What is the reason for everything – beyond the "great" black-white whole and beyond the unified zero-point energy field? God, you say? Then what is God and why does the Universe exist?

My mind cannot comprehend such profundity to attempt to answer these questions. However, when I ask my heart for the answer, I receive this swift reply – love. Love is at the heart of everything and beats within the heart of creation, just as it does within each of us.

Connecting to the Heart of Creation

The heart of creation beats without sound, without movement, and without effort. All motion is held within it. All sound is contained within its walls. All force and all energy originate there. All physical and non-physical matter resides within it. All light and life emanate from its eternal spiraling wave. Yet, the heart of the heart of creation holds nothing.

Love is a spiraling fractal. At the heart of everything is another heart. Within that heart, there is another heart. And so on. Even the highest powered telescope cannot locate love and the most powerful microscope cannot see its most intricate beauty. No biologist can dissect it, no chemist can formulate it, and no mathematician can solve its equation. No human eyes have looked upon it and no mind has comprehended its enormity. Love, like endless beauty, infinite wisdom, and unlimited power, cannot be contained and, therefore, cannot be defined.

Over the centuries, many people have tried to define love. Rumi, a famous thirteenth-century Persian poet and Sufi mystic, was noted for his poems about love and his love for God. Yet his heartfelt telling of his deep love for the divine still did not adequately define love. Since the notion of love is so vast and all encompassing, how can it be defined? Ever-changing yet constant, love is the great mystery. No single thing can define love. Its definition is as elusive as God's. The closest we can come to defining love is to describe its qualities.

Love is part of every aspect of the Universe. It is timelessness and formlessness existing in time and space. Love is woven within the fabric of time and space, within the zero-point energy field of the torus-shaped Universe. It is important to understand that love is not just the unified field; it is the *reason* for the field.

Love is the cause and purpose for everything. Love is the prime mover, the progenitor of all of creation. As such, it is the greatest force in the Universe.

Love is the in-breath and out-breath of the Universe, the ebb and flow of all things, such as the seasons and the tides. It creates every cycle in the Universe. The Universe operates under cosmic or universal laws, such as the law of cause and effect and the law of attraction, for which love is their origin and basis. At every level of creation – from galaxies to planets to people and to atoms – love is the guiding principle.

Love is ubiquitous, infinite, and expansive, without beginning or end, incessantly moving like a spiraling caduceus. Love, like energy, can neither be created nor destroyed. It has no opposites and cannot be replicated. Love just is.

Love is transcendent and multidimensional. It exists in all ways, at all times, and in all places. Death cannot erase it, miles cannot destroy it, and time cannot obliterate it.

Love exists without condition. Nothing can limit it. Nothing came before it. No force can conquer it. Love exists as the ever-increasing superlative nature of divine wisdom.

The cosmic mind, the unified consciousness of the Universe, operates through love. Love is the river through which higher consciousness flows. When we think with our hearts and come from love, we act from a higher consciousness or frequency. Pure love is the highest vibration of the Universe and the highest octave of harmonic expression.

Love is the sacred song of the cosmos, the Music of the Spheres, harmonically creating divine proportion according to the Golden Mean Ratio. Love is God's architect. All of creation is perfectly proportioned, creating what we define as beauty. Wherever love is present, coherence is promoted.

Love is responsible for the way everything is created. It is responsible for all attractive forces of the Universe; not just attraction between people, but attraction between particles as well. Love creates a cohesive Universe, holding planets in their orbits and atoms together to form molecules. Perhaps gravity, the weak force, covalent bonds and the like are nothing more than perturbations of manifest love.

Love is natural and supernatural. It is so interwoven into the natural world that it dwells within all life. Life is love in motion. Love is the body, the mind and its thoughts, every emotion, every breath, and the animating force behind all life. Love is also supernatural. It is not controlled by natural law since it is the cause for all laws in the Universe.

Love is all-inclusive: It cannot be separated. The aggregate and the one must exist simultaneously for either to have meaning. A grain of sand by itself does not define a beach, and a beach cannot exist without the individuation of a grain of sand. So it is with all of creation, expressing itself as unified diversity. Love knows only oneness. Essentially there is only one thing, love. Love really does make the world go around.

Everything is designed to promote love. Every nebula, galaxy, solar system, planet, being, and atom is programmed by love. Everything happens for a reason and that reason is, ultimately, love. No matter what happens, whether in the Universe or in our own lives, it happens because of love. God creates through love.

The Universe conspires for us: Every program was written with our best interest at heart. Water, for example, the Silly Putty* of the Universe, imprints messages from light and transfers those messages to us to promote our consciousness. Light, the chameleon of the Universe, is so intelligent that it is able to change its appearance from a wave to a particle. This physical flip-flop affects how accessible light is within our bodies, allowing us to become enlightened. No matter where you look in the Universe, from galaxy to gluon, love's wisdom reigns supreme.

Love is the great governor of the Universe, regulating and dispensing its grace to all. The heart of creation beats in unison with all that is. *"The Lord is my shepherd; I shall not want"* (Psalm 23, KJV). The Universe provides whatever we need – from challenges, to heartbreaks, to accomplishments, to joyous times. There is only love: What need have we of fear?

Love is a state of being. We cannot "do" love nor can we see love. We can only see the effects of love. Love is not a physical thing. It has the qualities of a wave of energy. As such, it can be felt within the heart, the body's most electromagnetic organ.

Connecting to the Human Heart

The truth of love can only be found by looking within the heart. The heart holds the timeless secrets of love for it is through the heart that we connect to all that is. Love enters and exits our physical body through the sacred coordinate within our heart. It permeates every organ, cell, and atom but it does not call any one of these its home within the body. Not even the heart can contain the enormity of love: It merely translates the language of love.

We are born with everything we need to love and be loved. Our sacred coordinate comes with its own USB connection: We are hardwired to communicate with the Universe. How we are raised, what we are taught, the friends we keep, our parents' beliefs, and how we are loved and cared for when we are young – all affect how open our heart becomes. A closed heart is worse than a closed mind because it hinders the flow of the highest form of intelligence in the Universe, love.

The heart is love's gateway. Only an open heart can allow love to enter or exit. The degree to which this divine doorway is open regulates the amount of love that can flow. A fully open heart allows an unencumbered and unlimited flow of love. It allows love to permeate every aspect of our being and our life. An open heart is full of love but it is not a vessel for love. The unlimited flow of love continuously keeps the heart full, yet the heart cannot contain love. Love is unending flow, perpetual motion. It cannot be contained. Love exists within everything yet resides nowhere.

A closed heart restricts the flow of love. It closes one off from others and the rest of the world. It isolates, constricts, and represses its owner. The heart's light becomes dim. Information carried by the light is limited, which curtails increasing consciousness, leading to further closing of the heart. The thought of loving oneself rarely comes up. A self-defeating cycle is created.

Loving yourself is the key to unlocking the doorway to your heart. At the heart of the human heart is self-love. The most important person to love or receive love is you. Self-realization is an inside job that cannot succeed without self-love. When we listen to what others tell us about ourselves, whether the source is television, radio, internet, friends, family, church, co-workers, government, etc., we neglect to listen to the most important voice of all: the one that comes from our own hearts. Self-love means honoring and respecting ourselves enough to put *our* thoughts and feelings first. It also requires us to fully embrace our human flaws while celebrating our divine perfection.

Each of us is a valuable part of creation, with our own set of gifts waiting to be shared with the world. All "gifts from God" come through the heart. Love is the giver and only the heart can accept such a gift. We use our gift every time we follow the promptings of our heart. When we follow our heart, we live our truth and express our divine unique-ness in the world. True self-love may look something like this: *"Here I am world, in my unique splendor, doing what my heart calls me to do, regardless of what anyone else may think. This is why I came, to share my unique gift with the world and to live in joy, because doing what I love brings me joy and I know I am meant to live joyfully."* Our hearts open wide when we unconditionally love, accept, and celebrate who we truly are.

The strength of the heart's electromagnetic field of an open-hearted person is so strong that there is a glow about them. As our heart allows more light to enter, the influx of information allows our consciousness to expand. Our love for life and everything in it is contagious. We become magnetic and attract what we need to carry out our heart's bidding. A cycle of increasing joy, abundance, gratitude, and love is created. We become "shining examples" of fully open-hearted people.

When we live in joy, our hearts are naturally open. We remember our natural state and allow love to guide us. We "beam with joy" because our heart-light is shining through. We glow. We become super-radiant, the true sign of an open heart.

If God creates through love, then living as the god that we are requires us to create through love. It also requires us to have an open heart. The Universe has a series of checks and balances to ensure that only those with open hearts wield the most creative power. Self-love is the key to successfully maneuvering through these checks and balances.

We can follow all the steps to manifesting outlined in Chapter 13, Stairway to Heaven, but until we love who we are, we cannot access the true power of our heart's electromagnetic field. When we love ourselves, our hearts are open, allowing more light to enter. As more light enters our heart, the strength of its electromagnetic field increases, which increases the likelihood of manifesting our dreams. Self-love is the foundation for creating our desires.

Self-love is necessary for us to download our divinity. This includes loving our divine self as well as our human self. Rahm is the type of love that flows through our pineal high-heart heart gateway and our heart's sacred coordinate. Rahm flows when we love our human *and* divine selves unconditionally and only then do we radiate love.

We must love *all* of who we are in order to become the true co-creators that we are.

CHAPTER FIFTEEN

The Key to the Heart of Creation

The heart knows what no one else has seen.

— *CYCLOPEA*

You have just experienced an information download by reading this book. What does that feel like? By now your brain may be on tilt, your eyes may be on sensory overload, and your heart may feel like it wants to explode. There is no need to panic, just take a few deep breaths and allow this information to integrate and to inform your DNA.

After journeying to the heart of creation through your heart, it's good to sit and rest for a while. Waking up to the truth of who you are entails more than just one brief "aha" moment. Downloading your divinity takes work. After all, you are putting together each piece of data until your divine download is complete.

Once the download is complete, one more important step remains: You must fall in love with your divine essence. To love yourself as the god that you are is to love the god within with all your heart, with all your mind, and with all your spirit. As I wrote in *In the Key of Life,* *"Opening to oneness is about opening your heart to your true self. It's about falling in love with you. It is the experience of love made manifest in the most intimate way possible"* (Cerio 2007, 1). When you fall in love with the god that you are, you fall in love with all creation.

To live as the god that you are is a totally new paradigm. When you live as the god that you are, you live in harmony with God. You are a part of God, the One Source of All. You are God's hands, eyes, and heart. You are entrained to the coherent motion of the particles of creation. All of creation awaits your command.

Living as the god that I AM is living in the perfection of now. All that "matters" is now, for creation of matter happens in the moment of now. You know and accept that each moment is perfect. You have the power to manifest what you desire from your heart in each moment, ensuring that your best interest, and the best interest of all, is served.

If it is true that we create our reality, then it's time to take responsibility for it. I AM response-able. I AM in-powered. I AM god incarnate. I love who I AM! It's time for true self-empowerment.

Raising our consciousness and frequency fills our hearts with the truth of who we are. The heart is said to be full because once we acknowledge our real identity, we realize that everything lies within us. God, the zero-point energy field, cosmic consciousness – it is all within. We are part of the field that flows through us. This is why the mystics have told us that we are not separate from each other. This web of energy connects all of us through multitudes of swirling vortexes. As I wrote in *In the Key of Life*, *"The void you think you created is an illusion, for what could you be void of? The entire Universe rests within you and you in the Universe. What could you want"*? (Cerio 2007, 63)

Each of us holds a key to creating our heart's desire. First, we must unlock the door using this key. Our heart field is the doorway that needs unlocking; it is not the key. The key lies in living as the god that we are.

The key to the heart of creation is nothing more than finding within your heart the ultimate wisdom: You are divine. You are God in form. Words like trust and hope no longer have meaning, for you know you are never separate from Source. When you know and live as the god that you are, your heart is always full of potential, full of possibilities, full of joy, full of wonder, full of gratitude, and full of love.

Our Father –

The divine consciousness within the great black-white whole,
the zero-point energy field
Your god self

Who art in Heaven –

The Universe
The heaven within your heart, your sacred coordinate

Hallowed be thy name –

The 72 names of God, YHVH, EHYEH ASHER EHYEH, ELOWAH
*Your given name that references your unique coordinate in the
unified field*
The power of the Logos or Word

Thy kingdom come –

The realization that the unified field is within and without
Living from your sacred coordinate or God's USB Port
Congruency

Thy will be done –

Divine will
Your will in alignment with divine will

On Earth as it is in Heaven –

The holographic nature of the Universe
The will of your essential self in alignment with the physical

Give us this day our daily bread –
The knowledge and wisdom of truth through the light of consciousness
Knowledge and wisdom of our truth through our sacred coordinate,
our connection to heaven

And forgive us our trespasses –
When we do not come from our hearts
When our intent is not alignment with our unique coordinate
in the unified field

As we forgive those who trespass against us –
When others do not come from their hearts
When others' intentions are not in alignment with their unique
coordinate in the unified field

For thine is the kingdom –
Our sacred coordinate realized and hardwired to heaven
The balanced divine masculine and feminine within
Congruency

The power –
The zero-point energy, the great black-white whole
The power of the Universe within us
The son/sun of God that we are

And the glory –
Omnipresent, omniscient, omnipotent unified field
The physical embodiment of the divine intelligence
Enlightenment

Forever –
Infinite without end
Eternal

Amen.
And so it is.

Afterword

Welcome home to your essence,
to the core of your being,
to the heart of who you are.

— *CYCLOPEA*

How does it feel to be a co-creator with all that is? Now that you know about your sacred coordinate, you have a lifetime gate pass to creation. *Everything you need can be accessed through your sacred coordinate.* You are hardwired to the One Source of All and all its creation. Therefore, you shall not want. When you live as the god that you are, you put an end to all kinds of poverty – in your life and in others' lives. This, my friends, is true freedom.

This freedom comes with a price: your commitment to your god self. It requires practice and patience, diligence and devotion, until living as the god that you are comes as easily and naturally as breathing.

Practice the meditations daily and perform the steps to create. Be patient with your progress. Becoming the god that you are rarely happens overnight. Be diligent about your choice of words, thoughts, and deeds. Ask yourself, is this how my god self speaks, thinks, and acts? Devote your whole heart to the process. Desire it above all else, and most importantly, love the god that you are with all your heart.

We know we are changing at every level of our being. The world as we have known it is also changing. Change is constant and a necessary part of growth but the change that we are experiencing is far greater than humanity has ever experienced. We are just now waking up to the truth of who we are.

We are the *co*-creators of our new world. Each of us does not live alone on an island. We are entering an era of *co*operation instead of competition because we realize what we do affects everything and everyone. Waking up to these truths is the only way we will create a lasting society built on trust, love, and respect for one another.

As the "heartless" world continues to topple, it is up to us, the co-creators of our world, to rebuild it from our hearts. If we are to thrive instead of just survive this monumental change, we must use the heart's intelligence to guide our way. When we create from our hearts and not our minds alone, we create a harmonic world. The heart creates from the perfection of the divine principle, love.

We are love in motion. The love that we are is upgraded every time we access Source through our sacred coordinates. Through this inter-dimensional cardiac connection, we gain access to the never-ending spiral of love. Our hearts are an unlimited resource of love, light, and wisdom. We cannot download our divinity without first connecting heaven's USB cable to our hearts.

In what may be humanity's hour of greatest need, may we all download our divinity and co-create a new Earth from our hearts – our hardwired connection to heaven.

References

CHAPTER ONE – TIMING IS EVERYTHING

Ventura, Carlo and Rollin McCraty. 2013. "DNA and Cell Reprogramming via Epigenetic Information Delivered by Magnetic Fields, Sound Vibration and Coherent Water." *Institute of HeartMath*. Accessed April 22, 2013. http://www. heartmath.org/free-services/downloads/dna-and-cell-reprogramming.html.

NASA. 2013. "Solar Cycle Update: Twin Peaks?" Accessed April 2, 2013. http://science.nasa.gov/science-news/science-at-nasa/2013/01mar_twinpeaks.

Phys.org. 2010. "Evidence of second fast north-south pole flip found." Accessed February 10, 2012. http://phys.org/news202971192.html. See also **Bogue, Scott W. and Jonathan M. G. Glen. 2010.** "Very rapid geomagnetic field change recorded by the partial remagnetization of a lava flow." *Geophysical Research Letters* 37: 1-5. Accessed February 10, 2012. doi: 10.1029/2010GL044286.

Lungold, Ian. 2005. Lecture on the Mayan Calendar. Sedona, Arizona, January 21.

CHAPTER TWO – A 'HOLE' NEW WORLD

Haramein, Nassim. 2010. Lecture presented at the annual Science and Nonduality Conference, San Rafael, California, October 20 – 24.

Hameroff, Stuart. 1987. *Ultimate Computing: Biomolecular Consciousness and Nanotechnology.* Amsterdam: Elsevier Science Publishers. See also **McTaggart, Lynne. 2002.** *The Field: The Quest for the Secret Force of the Universe*. New York: Harper Collins Publishers.

Haramein, Nassim. 2010. Lecture presented at the annual Science and Nonduality Conference, San Rafael, California, October 20 – 24.

Jibu, Mari, Scott Hagan, Stuart R. Hameroff, Karl H. Pribram, and Kunio Yasue. 1994. "Quantum optical coherence in cytoskeletal microtubules: implications for brain function." *Biosystems* 32: 195-209.

Popp, Fritz-Albert, Qiao Gu, and Ke-Hsueh Li. 1994. "Biophoton emission: Experimental background and theoretical approaches." *Modern Physics Letters B* 8: 1269-1296.

Ibid.

McTaggart, Lynne. 2002. *The Field: The Quest for the Secret Force of the Universe*. New York: Harper Collins Publishers.

CHAPTER THREE – A CREATIVE ENERGY STORY

Haramein, Nassim. 2010. Lecture presented at the annual Science and Nonduality Conference, San Rafael, California, October 20 – 24.

CHAPTER FOUR – THE HEART OF MATTER

Dartmouth College. 2013. "Shedding new light on the brightest objects in the universe." Science*Daily*. Accessed July 24, 2013. http://www.sciencedaily. com/releases/2013/07/130724200605.htm?utm_source=feedburner&utm_ medium=feed&utm_campaign=Feed%3A+sciencedaily+%28ScienceDaily%3A+ Latest+Science+News%29.

Wanjek, Christopher. 2006. "NASA Scientists Determine the Nature of Black Hole Jets." NASA Goddard Space Flight Center. Accessed July 24, 2013. http://www. nasa.gov/centers/goddard/news/topstory/2006/swift_blazars.html.

Haramein, Nassim. 2010. Lecture presented at the annual Science and Nonduality Conference, San Rafael, California, October 20 – 24.

Ibid.

Schwenk, Theodor. Reprinted 2008. Rev. translation 1996. *Sensitive Chaos: The Creation of Flowing Forms in Water and Air.* East Sussex: Rudolph Steiner Press.

Buckberg, Gerald, MD; Julien I. E. Hoffman, MD; Aman Mahajan, MD; Saleh Saleh, MD; and Cecil Coghlan, MD. 2008. "Cardiac Mechanics Revisited. The Relationship of Cardiac Architecture to Ventricular Function." *Circulation* 118: 2571-2587. Accessed July 26, 2013. doi: 10.1161/CIRCULATIONA-HA.107.754424.

Besant, Annie and Charles W. Leadbeater. 1919. Occult Chemistry: Clairvoyant Observations on the Chemical Elements. Revised edition edited by A. P. Sinnett. London: Theosophical Publishing House.

Cerio, Joan. 2007. *In the Key of Life: An Activational Journey to the Soul.* Sedona: Life Lines.

Cantin, M., J. Gutkowska, G. Thiabault, R. Garcia, M. Anand-Srivastava, P. Hamet, E. Schiffrin, and J. Genest. 1984. "The Heart as an Endocrine Gland." *Journal of the International Society of Hypertension* 2: 329-331.

American Physiological Society. February 25, 2008 Press Release. "Taking the Fight Against Cancer to Heart." Accessed February 27, 2012. http://www.the-aps. org/mm/hp/Audiences/Public-Press/For-the-Press/releases/Archive/08/4.html.

Buhner, Stephen Harrod. 2004. *The Secret Teaching of Plants: The Intelligence of the Heart in the Direct Perception of Nature*. Rochester: Bear & Company.

Ibid.

McCraty, Rollin, Raymond Trevor Bradley, and Dana Tomasino. 2004-5. "The Resonant Heart." *Shift: The Frontiers of Consciousness,* December-February.

McCraty, Rollin, Mike Atkinson, and Dana Tomasino. 2001. "Science of the Heart: Exploring the Role of the Heart in Human Performance." *Institute of HeartMath*. Accessed February 27, 2012. http://www.heartmath.org/research/ science-of-the-heart/introduction.html.

McCraty, Rollin, Raymond Trevor Bradley, and Dana Tomasino. 2004-5. "The Resonant Heart." *Shift: The Frontiers of Consciousness,* December-February.

CHAPTER FIVE – BLOOD & WATER

Hurtak, JJ. 3rd ed. 1987. *The Book of Knowledge: The Keys of Enoch*. Los Gatos: The Academy for Future Science.

NASA. 2011. "Astronomers Find Largest Most Distant Reservoir of Water." NASA Mission News. Accessed February 27, 2012. http://www.nasa.gov/topics/universe/features/universe20110722.html. See also **Bradford, C. M., A. D. Bolatto, P. R. Maloney, J. E. Aguirre, J. J. Bock, J. Glenn, J. Kamenetzky, R. Lupu, H. Matsuhara, E. J. Murphy, B. J. Naylor, H. T. Nguyen, K. Scott, and J. Zmuidzinas. 2011**. "The Water Vapor Spectrum of APM 08279+5255: X-Ray Heating and Infrared Pumping over Hundreds of Parsecs." *The Astrophysical Journal Letters* 741: 1-6. Accessed February 27, 2012. doi:10.1088/2041-8205/741/2/L37.

Schwenk, Theodor. Reprinted 2008. Rev. translation 1996. *Sensitive Chaos: The Creation of Flowing Forms in Water and Air.* East Sussex: Rudolph Steiner Press.

Masaru Emoto. 2010. "Dr. Masaru Emoto." Accessed July 15, 2013. http://masaru-emoto.net/english/emoto.html.

Schiff, Michel. 1995. *The Memory of Water: Homoeopathy and the Battle of Ideas in the New Science.* Northampton: Thorsons.

Davenas, E., F. Beauvais, J. Amara, M. Oberbaum, B. Robinzon, A. Miadonna, A. Tedeschi, B. Pomeranz, P. Fortner, P. Belon, J. Sainte-Laudy, B. Poitevin, and J. Benveniste. 1988. "Human basophil degranulation triggered by very dilute antiserum against IgE." *Nature* 333: 816-18.

Lipton, Bruce PhD. 2005. *The Biology of Belief: Unleashing the Power of Consciousness, Matter, & Miracles.* Santa Rosa: Mountain of Love/Elite Books.

Hurtak, JJ. 3rd ed 1987. *The Book of Knowledge: The Keys of Enoch*. Los Gatos: The Academy for Future Science.

Prophet, Mark L. and Elizabeth Clare Prophet. 2001. *The Masters and the Spiritual Path.* Corwin Springs: Summit University Press.

Haramein, Nassim. Uploaded 2011. *We are the Center of Creation Part 2 of 2 Interview* on SupremeMasterTV14.com. Accessed February 28, 2012. http://www.youtube.com/watch?v=twq8NY2kb-0.

Jibu, Mari, Scott Hagan, Stuart R. Hameroff, Karl H. Pribram, and KunioYasue. 1994. "Quantum optical coherence in cytoskeletal microtubules: implications for brain function." *Biosystems* 32: 195-209.

Braden, Gregg. 1997 rev. ed. *Awakening to Zero Point: The Collective Initiation.* Bellevue: Radio Bookstore Press. (If you have any questions about Mr. Braden's work, please contact M. Lauri Willmot, Executive Director, Wisdom Traditions, Office of Gregg Braden, PO Box 14668, North Palm Beach, FL 33408, 561-799-9337.)

CHAPTER SIX – THE SACRED COORDINATE ... GOD'S USB PORT

Green, Glenda. Rev. ed 2002. *Love Without End - Jesus Speaks.* Sedona: Spirits Publishing.

Haramein, N., and E. A. Rauscher. 2005. "The origin of spin: A consideration of torque and coriolis forces in Einstein's field equations and grand unification theory." In *Beyond the Standard Model: Searching for Unity in Physics*, edited by Richard L. Amoroso, Bo Lehnert, and Jean-Pierre Vigier. The Noetic Press, 153-168.

Schucman, Helen. 1996. *A Course in Miracles.* Mill Valley: The Foundation for Inner Peace.

Cerio, Joan. 2007. *In the Key of Life: An Activational Journey to the Soul.* Sedona: Life Lines.

Bearden, Thomas. (no year given). "Extracting and using electromagnetic energy from the active vacuum." Accessed February 25, 2012. http://cheniere.org/tech-papers/bearden4.pdf.

Bearden, Thomas. 2000. "Giant Negentropy from the Common Dipole." Accessed February 25, 2012. http://www.cheniere.org/techpapers/GiantNegentropy.pdf.

Puthoff, H. A. 1989. "Source of vacuum electromagnetic zero-point energy." *Physical Review A* 40: 4857-4862.

Sereda, David. 2008. "Amazing Water" Radio Interview on *Coast to Coast with George Noory AM* as found on YouTube. Accessed March 3, 2012. http://www.youtube.com/watch?v=tW5KkTokPSQ.

Clare Prophet, Elizabeth. 2010. *Becoming God: The Path of the Christian Mystic.* Gardiner: Summit University Press.

Staveley-Smith, Lister and Bryan Gaensler. 2013. "Galactic geysers fuelled by star stuff." *International Centre for Radio Astronomy Research.* Accessed July 1, 2013. http://www.icrar.org/news/news_items/media-releases/galactic-geysers-fuelled-by-star-stuff.

Cerio, Joan. 2007. *In the Key of Life: An Activational Journey to the Soul.* Sedona: Life Lines.

CHAPTER SEVEN – TURNING ON YOUR HEART'S LIGHT

Cerio, Joan. 2007. *In the Key of Life: An Activational Journey to the Soul.* Sedona: Life Lines.

Rohde, Robert and Richard Muller. 2005. "Cycles in fossil diversity." *Nature* 434: 208-210. Accessed July 1, 2013. doi: 10.1038/nature03339.

Wilcock, David. 2011. *The Source Field Investigations* video. Accessed March 3, 2012. http://divinecosmos.com/start-here/davids-blog/959-sourcefieldvideo.

Miller, Robert J. 1994. *The Complete Gospels.* Sonoma: Polebridge Press. (Quote used with permission from publisher)

Green, Glenda. Rev. ed. 2002. *Love Without End - Jesus Speaks.* Sedona: Spirits Publishing.

Ibid.

CHAPTER EIGHT – EYE AM

Strassman, Rick. 2001. *DMT: The Spirit Molecule, A Doctor's Revolutionary Research into the Biology of Near-Death and Mystical Experiences.* Rochester: Park Street Press.

Ibid.

Silva, Freddy. 2002. *Secrets in the Fields: The Science and Mysticism of Crop Circles.* Charlottesville: Hampton Roads Publishing.

NIH News Press Release. August 12, 2004. "Pineal Gland Evolved To Improve Vision, According To Theory By NICHD Scientist." http://www.nih.gov/news/pr/aug2004/nichd-12.htm. See also **Klein, David C. 2004.** "The 2004 Aschoff/Pittendrigh Lecture: Theory of the Origin of the Pineal Gland—A Tale of Conflict and Resolution." *Journal of Biological Rhythms* 19: 264. Accessed July 23, 2013. doi:10.1177/0748730404267340.

Wilcock, David. 2011. *The Source Field Investigations* video. Accessed March 3, 2012. http://divinecosmos.com/start-here/davids-blog/959-sourcefieldvideo.

Bayliss, C. R., N. L. Bishop, and R. C. Fowler. 1985. "Pineal gland calcification and defective sense of direction." *British Medical Journal.* 291: 1758-1759.

Wilcock, David. 2011. *The Source Field Investigations* video. Accessed March 3, 2012. http://divinecosmos.com/start-here/davids-blog/959-sourcefieldvideo.

Oprah Winfrey Network. 2011. "The Science of Consciousness." *Miracle Detectives.* Accessed March 3, 2012. http://www.oprah.com/own-miracle-detectives/The-Science-of-Consciousness.

Montagnier, L., J. Aïssa, E. Del Giudice, C. Lavallée, A. Tedeschi, and G. Vitiello. 2010. "DNA waves and water." Paper presented at the DICE2010 Conference, Castiglioncello, Italy, September.

Montagnier, Luc, Jamal Aïssa, Stéphane Ferris, Jean-Luc Montagnier, and Claude Lavallée. 2009. "Electromagnetic Signals are Produced by Aqueous Nanostructures Derived from Bacterial DNA Sequences." *Interdisciplinary Sciences: Computational Life Sciences* 1: 81-90. Accessed July 16, 2013. doi: 10.1007/s12539-009-0036-7.

Khesbak, Hassan, Olesya Savchuk, Satoru Tsushima, and Karim Fahmy. 2011. "The Role of Water H-Bond Imbalance in B-DNA Substrate Transitions and Peptide Recognition Revealed by Time-Resolved FTIR Spectroscopy." *Journal of the American Chemical Society* 133: 5834-5842.

Harvard-Smithsonian Center for Astrophysics Press Release No: 2013-19. July 17, 2013. "Earth's Gold Came from Colliding Dead Stars." Accessed July 20, 2013. http://www.cfa.harvard.edu/news/2013/pr201319.html.

Gutkowska, Jolanta, Marek Janowski, Chantal Lambert, Suhayla Mukaddam-Daher, Hans H. Zingg, and Samuel M. McCann. 1997. "Oxcytocin releases atrial natriuretic peptide by combining with oxytocin receptors in the heart." *Proceedings of the National Academy of Sciences USA* 94: 11704-11709.

Douglas-Klotz, Neil. 2001. *The Hidden Gospel: Decoding the Spiritual Message of the Aramaic Jesus*. Wheaton: Quest Books.

CHAPTER NINE – HOW CREATIVE ENERGY WORKS

McCraty, Rollin, and Doc Childre. 2010. "Coherence: bridging personal, social, and global health." *Alternative Therapies* 16: 10-24.

Ibid.

Schwenk, Theodor. Reprinted 2008. Rev. translation 1996. *Sensitive Chaos: The Creation of Flowing Forms in Water and Air*. East Sussex: Rudolph Steiner Press.

Hurtak, JJ. 3rd ed. 1987. *The Book of Knowledge: The Keys of Enoch˚*. Los Gatos: The Academy for Future Science.

Douglas-Klotz, Neil. 2001. *The Hidden Gospel: Decoding the Spiritual Message of the Aramaic Jesus*. Wheaton: Quest Books.

Bearden, Thomas. 2000. "Giant Negentropy from the Common Dipole." Accessed February 25, 2012. http://www.cheniere.org/techpapers/GiantNegentropy. pdf. See also Whittaker, E. T. 1903. "On the Partial Differential Equations of Mathematical Physics." *Mathematische Annalen*. 53: 333-355.

CHAPTER TEN – BLUEPRINTS OF CREATION

Hill, Napoleon. 2012. *The Law of Success: The 16 Secrets for Achieving Wealth & Prosperity*. Mineola: Dover Publications, Inc. (Quoted from p.77 by permission of publisher)

McTaggart, Lynne. 2002. *The Field: The Quest for the Secret Force of the Universe*. New York: Harper Collins Publishers.

Prophet, Mark L. and Elizabeth Clare Prophet. 2001. *The Masters and the Spiritual Path*. Corwin Springs: Summit University Press.

Braden, Gregg. 1997 rev. ed. *Awakening to Zero Point: The Collective Initiation*. Bellevue: Radio Bookstore Press. (If you have any questions about Mr. Braden's work, please contact M. Lauri Willmot, Executive Director, Wisdom Traditions, Office of Gregg Braden, PO Box 14668, North Palm Beach, FL 33408, 561-799-9337.)

CHAPTER ELEVEN – ALIGNING WITH THE DIVINE

Robinson, James McConley. 1977. *The Nag Hammadi Library: Translated into English under the Editorship of James M. Robinson*. Leiden: E. J. Brill. (Quoted from p. 121 by permission of publisher)

Green, Glenda. Rev. ed. 2002. *Love Without End - Jesus Speaks*. Sedona: Spirits Publishing.

Prophet, Mark L. and Elizabeth Clare Prophet. 2001. *The Masters and the Spiritual Path*. Corwin Springs: Summit University Press.

Miller, Robert J. 1994. *The Complete Gospels*. Sonoma: Polebridge Press. (Quote used with permission from publisher)

Braden, Gregg. 1997 rev. ed. *Awakening to Zero Point: The Collective Initiation*.

Bellevue: Radio Bookstore Press. (If you have any questions about Mr. Braden's work, please contact M. Lauri Willmot, Executive Director, Wisdom Traditions, Office of Gregg Braden, PO Box 14668, North Palm Beach, FL 33408, 561-799-9337.)

Schwenk, Theodor. Reprinted 2008. Rev. translation 1996. *Sensitive Chaos: The Creation of Flowing Forms in Water and Air.* East Sussex: Rudolph Steiner Press.

Bearden, Thomas. 2000. "Giant Negentropy from the Common Dipole." Accessed February 25, 2012. http://www.cheniere.org/techpapers/GiantNegentropy.pdf.

CHAPTER TWELVE – TOOLS FOR CREATION

Cerio, Joan. 2007. *In the Key of Life: An Activational Journey to the Soul.* Sedona: Life Lines.

CHAPTER FIFTEEN – THE KEY TO THE HEART OF CREATION

Cerio, Joan. 2007. *In the Key of Life: An Activational Journey to the Soul.* Sedona: Life Lines.

Ibid.

About the Author

As an author, teacher, speaker, and healer, and the founder of the Coeuressence School of Self-Mastery, Joan Cerio has crossed the United States multiple times, sharing her gifts and insights with groups and in one-on-one sessions, and helping many to awaken to the gods that they are. Coeuressence was sparked by Joan's first book, *In the Key of Life: An Activational Journey to the Soul*, and its work has deepened as a result of *Hardwired to Heaven*.

Joan has been involved with the health and healing professions for more than thirty years. In addition to creating Integrative Message Therapy, she has also worked as a massage therapist, Reiki master teacher, integrated energy therapy practitioner, and intuitive sound healer.

Joan holds a graduate degree in science education and an undergraduate degree in biology, which, together, contribute to the conceptual and energetic balance between the physical and spiritual in her life. She has taught secondary science, massage therapy and Reiki, and, through Coeuressence, continues to teach a wide variety of metaphysical and self-realization workshops. Her ability to bridge the worlds of science and metaphysics has also made her a popular guest on a variety of radio shows.

For more information about Joan, and her work, please visit:
www.Joancerio.com
She also has a dedicated site for this book:
www.hardwiredtoheaven.com

F I N D H O R N   P R E S S

Life Changing Books

Findhorn Press Ltd
117-121 High Street,
Forres IV36 1AB,
Scotland, UK

t +44 (0)1309 690582
f +44 (0)131 777 2711
e info@findhornpress.com

or consult our catalogue online
(with secure order facility) on
www.findhornpress.com

For information on the Findhorn Foundation:
www.findhorn.org